EYEWITNESS
ANCIENT
GREECE

Bronze mirror cover showing Aphrodite playing Jacks with Pan (350 BCE)

Round-mouthed pitcher with coins

Griffin's head *oinochoe*

Bronze banqueter figurine

Aphrodite fastening her sandal

Theseus and the Minotaur

Kylix

Bronze
chariot
ornament

EYEWITNESS
ANCIENT
GREECE

Written by
ANNE PEARSON

Oil container

Wine strainer

Bronze cymbals

DK

LONDON, NEW YORK,
MELBOURNE, MUNICH, AND DELHI

Project editor Gillian Denton
Art editor Liz Sephton
Senior editor Helen Parker
Senior art editor Julia Harris
Production Louise Barratt
Picture research Diana Morris
Special photography Nick Nicolls
Additional photography Liz MacCaulay

RELAUNCH EDITION (DK UK)
Editor Ashwin Khurana
US editor Margaret Parrish
Senior designers Rachael Grady, Spencer Holbrook
Managing editor Gareth Jones
Managing art editor Philip Letsu
Publisher Andrew Macintyre
Producer, preproduction Adam Stoneham
Senior producer Charlotte Cade
Jacket editor Maud Whatley
Jacket designer Laura Brim
Jacket design development manager Sophia MTT
Publishing director Jonathan Metcalf
Associate publishing director Liz Wheeler
Art director Phil Ormerod

RELAUNCH EDITION (DK INDIA)
Editors Surbhi Nayyar Kapoor, Priyanka Kharbanda
Art editors Deep Shikha Walia, Dhirendra Singh
Senior DTP designer Harish Aggarwal
DTP designers Anita Yadav, Pawan Kumar
Managing editor Alka Thakur Hazarika
Managing art editor Romi Chakraborty
CTS manager Balwant Singh
Jacket editorial manager Saloni Talwar
Jacket designers Govind Mittal, Suhita Dharamjit, Vidit Vashisht

First American Edition, 1992
This American Edition, 2014

Published in the United States by DK Publishing
4th floor, 345 Hudson Street
New York, New York 10014
14 15 16 17 18   10 9 8 7 6 5 4 3 2 1
196430—07/14

A catalog record for this book is available from the Library of Congress.
ISBN 978-1-4654-2049-7 (Paperback)
ISBN 978-1-4654-2091-6 (ALB)

DK books are available at special discounts when purchased in bulk
for sales promotions, premiums, fund-raising, or educational use.
For details, contact: DK Publishing Special Markets, 345 Hudson Street,
New York, New York 10014 or SpecialSale@dk.com.

Color reproduction by Alta Image Ltd., London, UK
Printed and bound by South China Printing Co. Ltd., China

Discover more at
www.dk.com

**Terra-cotta
dancing
woman**

**Terra-cotta
figurine of a
youth with hat**

**Griffin
earrings**

**Rattle
shaped
like a pig**

Contents

Child's toy

Greek world

The country of Greece is made up of a mountainous mainland and hundreds of islands scattered throughout the Aegean and Adriatic seas. Early Greek settlements grew as small, rival communities called city-states, which were cut off from each other by mountains and the sea. Each city-state had its own identity and its citizens were very loyal to their home state and its patron god. The ancient Greeks created one of the world's most advanced civilizations, leading the way in literature, philosophy, sports, theater, and politics. Greek civilization reached its peak in the city of Athens in the fifth century BCE.

The British Museum
Built in the 19th century, the British Museum in London, UK, was inspired by classical Greek architecture. Many of the objects in this book can be seen there.

Kouros
Kouroi (marble statues of naked boys) were mainly used to decorate the sanctuaries of the gods. Others were dedicated to young soldiers killed in battle. The statues stand with one foot forward.

The Greek world
This map shows ancient Greece and its early settlements abroad. A need for land drove many ancient Greeks to leave the mainland. Some traveled east and settled on the Ionian coast of Asia Minor. The names of the regions are in capitals and the cities are in small letters.

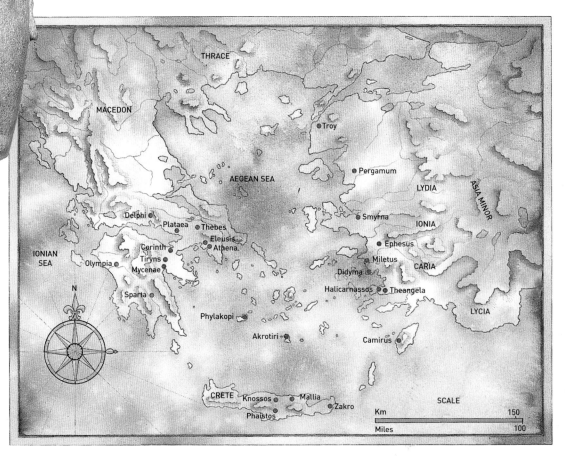

THRACE

MACEDON

Troy

AEGEAN SEA

Pergamum

LYDIA

ASIA MINOR

Delphi
Plataea
Thebes
Eleusis
Athena.
Corinth
Tiryns
Mycenae

Smyrna

IONIA

Ephesus

Miletus

CARIA

Didyma

IONIAN SEA

Olympia

Sparta

Halicarnassos
Theangela

LYCIA

Phylakopi

N

Akrotiri

Camirus

CRETE
Knossos
Mallia
Zakro
Phaistos

SCALE

Km   150
Miles   100

Acropolis

Centered around a hilltop fortress called the Acropolis, Athens (pp. 16–17) was the leading city in ancient Greece. Its most sacred temple, the Parthenon, was dedicated to the goddess Athena.

Donkey cup

The Greeks were famous for their beautifully painted pottery, used mainly for storing, mixing, and serving wine. This is a special two-handled cup in the form of a donkey's head.

Hippocamp

This gold ring is decorated with a hippocamp, a sea horse with two front feet and the tail of a dolphin or a fish.

Greece and the wider world

This chart shows the rise and fall of the Greek world from Minoan times to the end of the Hellenistic Age. These historic events can be seen against a background of other civilizations in Europe, Asia, and South America.

DATES BCE	2000–1500	1500–1100	1100–800	800–479	479–323	323–30
EVENTS IN GREECE	Cretan palace civilization	Fall of Knossos Rise and fall of Mycenaean civilization	Earliest Greek cities in Ionia	First Olympic Games Greek colonies in Black Sea/Sicily Persian invasions	Sparta controls Peloponnese Age of Perikles Rise of Macedon Life of Alexander	Wars of Alexander's successors Roman conquest
CULTURAL PERIOD	Bronze Age	Bronze Age	Early Iron Age	Archaic	Classical	Hellenistic
WORLD EVENTS	Indus Valley civilization in India Middle Kingdom in Egypt	Egyptian New Kingdom Hittite Empire Shang dynasty in China	Olmec civilization in Mexico Earliest Phoenician colonies	Rise of Etruscans in Italy Rome founded Assyrian Empire	Confucius born in China Buddha born in India Persian Empire	Qin and Han dynasties in China Mayan civilization in Central America

Marathon men

Track and field was a favorite pastime in ancient Greece (pp. 44–45). These runners were painted on a pot that was given as a prize in the Panathenaic Games held in Athens (pp. 16–17).

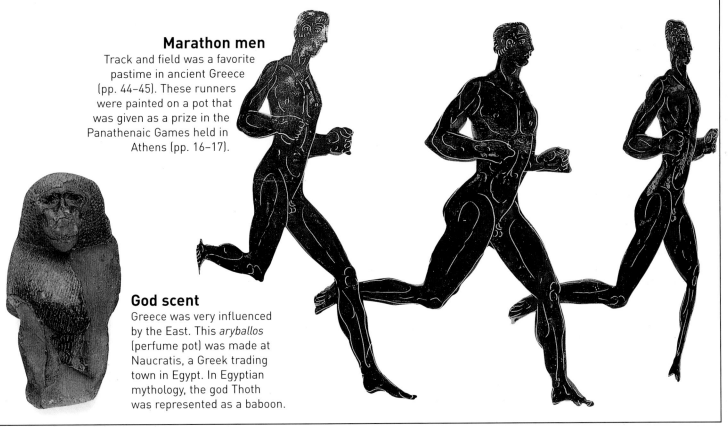

God scent

Greece was very influenced by the East. This *aryballos* (perfume pot) was made at Naucratis, a Greek trading town in Egypt. In Egyptian mythology, the god Thoth was represented as a baboon.

The Minoans

Decorating with dolphins
The Minoan palaces were decorated with frescoes, made by applying paint to wet plaster. This famous dolphin fresco is from the Queen's apartment at Knossos.

The island of Crete was home to Europe's first great civilization. The Minoans (named after Minos, a legendary king of Crete) settled as early as 6000 BCE, reaching the height of their powers between 2200 BCE and 1500 BCE. Crops flourished in the rich soil, and the Minoans grew wealthy from trade with other Bronze-Age towns. The Minoans built luxurious palaces in Greece, the most important of which was the palace of Knossos.

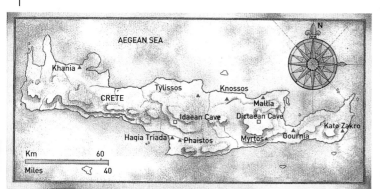

Worshiper
This bronze figure is worshiping the gods.

Crete
This map shows the sites of the main Minoan towns and palaces. It also shows the site of a large villa at Hagia Triada. Most settlements were built near the sea. Ordinary people lived in townhouses or on farms in the country. It is said that the god Zeus was raised in the Dictaean Cave on the Lassithi plain.

Taking the bull by the horns
Bulls were sacred to the Minoans and bull-leaping was probably a form of worship. According to myth, Zeus turned himself into a bull and swam to Crete with the princess Europa on his back. Their son, Minos, later became king of Crete. This bronze figure shows a boy somersaulting over a bull's horns.

Bull mural
This mural at Knossos also shows an acrobat leaping a bull.

Discovering Knossos

English archeologist Sir Arthur Evans (1851–1941) discovered the palace of Knossos in 1894. The remains showed that the palace contained hundreds of rooms.

Theseus and the Minotaur

According to legend, the Athenian prince Theseus went to Crete to kill a man-eating monster called the Minataur. Half-man and half-bull, the Minotaur was kept in a maze called the Labyrinth. The long, winding corridors at Knossos may have resembled a labyrinth.

Modern Minotaur

The story of the Minotaur has inspired many artists through the ages. This interpretation by Spanish artist Pablo Picasso (1881–1973) is almost as difficult to unravel as the maze!

Restoration

The palace of Knossos was rebuilt several times. Made of stone with wooden ceilings, some parts of it were four stories high. The royal apartments included a throne room where the ruler of Knossos sat in splendor. Sir Arthur Evans restored some of the palace to its former glory. The wooden columns are painted the same shade of red as the originals.

The Mycenaeans

During the Bronze Age, a warlike society developed around the Greek city of Mycenae. The Mycenaeans were great warriors and traders who lived in small kingdoms centered around heavily fortified palaces. The wealthy Mycenaean civilization reached its peak in about 1600 BCE. However, by around 1250 BCE the Mycenaean world was under threat from foreign invaders, and by around 1200 BCE their cities began to be abandoned or destroyed. Within a hundred years, the Mycenaean strongholds had fallen and a period called the Dark Ages had begun.

Pomegranate pendant
This gold pendant was found in Cyprus, where many Mycenaean artists and traders settled as their civilization crumbled. It was made by a Mycenaean craftsman in around 1300 BCE and is decorated with tiny gold granules grouped in triangles.

Bull sprinkler
This clay bull's head with small holes in its mouth was used to sprinkle water at religious ceremonies. The bull was the most common animal shape for these ritual sprinklers.

Octopus jar
This pottery jar decorated with an octopus was found in a cemetery at a Mycenaean colony on the island of Rhodes. Mycenaean artists were very influenced by Minoan artists, who often painted subjects inspired by the sea.

Grave circle

In 1876, Heinrich Schliemann (p. 12) excavated a royal burial ground at Mycenae. It contained tombs called shaft graves enclosed by a wall. The graves held vast amounts of gold jewelry that date from around 1600 BCE.

Lion Gate

The main entrance through Mycenae's city walls was a huge, stone gateway, decorated with the sculptures of two lions on either side of a pillar. This may have been the symbol of Mycenae's royal family.

View from the past

This engraving shows how the Lion Gate would have looked when it was first excavated. The lions had probably been displaced by an earthquake.

Fish cup

Mycenaean artists often worked for the king and built their workshops close to the palace. The shape of this long-stemmed cup, decorated with cuttlefish, was invented by the Mycenaeans.

Mask of Agamemnon

Five of the royal people buried in the Mycenaean shaft graves wore gold funeral masks. Heinrich Schliemann mistakenly believed that the death mask shown here belonged to Agamemnon, the legendary king of Mycenae during the Trojan War. It has since been dated to an earlier time.

Bird women

Thousands of little beak-nosed figures shaped like women have been found at Mycenaean sites. They may represent a fertility goddess.

To Troy and back

In the twelfth century BCE, the powerful Mycenaean civilization collapsed and Greece entered a dark age. During the next few centuries, stories of heroic Mycenaeans were handed down in the form of poems. Two of the most famous poems were written by the poet Homer in the eighth century BCE: *The Iliad* describes how the city of Troy was besieged by the army of King Agamemnon of Mycenae and *The Odyssey* describes the adventures of the Greek hero Odysseus on his return from the Trojan War. It is likely that the Greeks and Trojans did go to war, but over the ownership of land and crops, rather than the recapture of Helen (above).

Helen of Troy
Helen was the beautiful wife of Menelaus, king of Sparta and brother of King Agamemnon. According to legend, Helen was captured by Paris, son of Priam, king of Troy, This led to the Trojan War.

Heinrich Schliemann
In 1870, German archeologist Heinrich Schliemann (1822–90) discovered the ancient city of Troy on the coast of modern Turkey. The excavation revealed nine cities built on top of each other. Schliemann's wife is wearing jewelry found at the site.

Overcome by curiosity
After a 10-year siege, the Greeks tricked the Trojans by leaving a huge wooden horse outside Troy. Curious, the Trojans dragged it inside their city walls. That night, Greek soldiers, who were hiding inside the horse, crept out and let their army into Troy. This pot showing the horse is from about 625 BCE.

Modern model
In Troy today there is a modern replica of the Trojan horse. It is very large and, like the ancient one, is made of wood. Children can climb a ladder into its stomach and pretend to be Greek soldiers.

The wooden horse
Many artists have been inspired by the story of the Trojan horse. This painting is by Italian artist Giovanni Tiepolo (1696–1770).

The blinding of Polyphemus

One day, Odysseus met Polyphemus, a one eyed, man-eating giant who trapped Odysseus and his men in his cave, then began to eat them one by one. Cunning Odysseus brought the giant a skin full of wine to make him fall asleep. Then he blinded Polyphemus by driving a red-hot stake into his only eye.

Patient Penelope

After 10 years, Odysseus returned to his wife Penelope, who had waited patiently for him. Penelope had put off marriage proposals from other men, saying that she would reply only when she had finished her weaving. But every night, she undid all her work so that her weaving was never finished. This painting by British artist John Stanhope (1829–1908) shows Penelope sitting sadly beside her loom.

Woolly escape

Odysseus and his men escaped by tying themselves beneath a flock of sheep that Polyphemus kept in his cave overnight. In the morning, as the sheep left the cave, the blinded giant checked their woolly backs, but did not think of feeling under their bellies.

Blue paint indicating sea

Helmet

Mother to the rescue

Achilles' mother was a sea nymph named Thetis. This terra-cotta figurine shows Thetis on a seahorse bringing a new helmet for Achilles to wear in battle. Some of the bright blue paint representing the sea still survives.

Death of a hero

After the Greek champion Achilles had killed the bravest Trojan warrior, Hektor, he tied his body to a chariot and dragged it three times around the walls of Troy. On this clay lamp, Achilles is shown driving the chariot and looking back in triumph. Above him, Hektor's parents, King Priam and Queen Hecuba, watch in horror.

Golden griffins
These gold griffin heads, found on the island of Rhodes, were once part of a pair of earrings.

Greek expansion

Fond farewell
This detail is from a pot painted in the Greek Geometric style (a style based on geometric patterns). The figures, painted in silhouette, are rather rigid.

Greece started to emerge from the Dark Ages in the eighth century BCE. As the population grew, and more land and crops were needed, the Greeks started to set up colonies in southern Italy, Sicily, and along the shores of the Black Sea. At this time, Greek culture became influenced by designs from the east. The Greek geometric patterns were replaced by designs, such as griffins and sphinxes from Egypt and Syria. The Greek cities of Corinth, Rhodes, and Ephesus were well placed for trade with the east and became very wealthy.

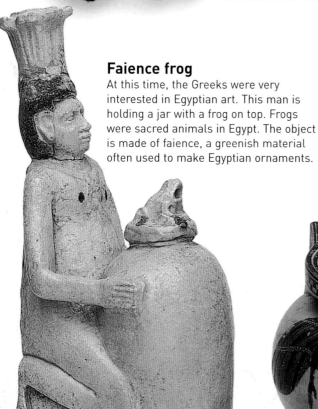

Man size
The Greeks liked to wear bangles decorated with animal heads. This lion-headed bangle, which is silver-plated, may have been worn by a man.

Faience frog
At this time, the Greeks were very interested in Egyptian art. This man is holding a jar with a frog on top. Frogs were sacred animals in Egypt. The object is made of faience, a greenish material often used to make Egyptian ornaments.

Lion pot
This *aryballos* (perfume pot) has a spout shaped like a lion's head. It has three painted scenes showing a warrior procession, a horse-race, and dogs chasing hares. The lion's mouth would have been filled with wax to stop the perfume from evaporating.

Exotic exports
Many decorated perfume pots were made in the town of Corinth and exported all over the Greek world. The winged figure on this pot may represent a god of the wind.

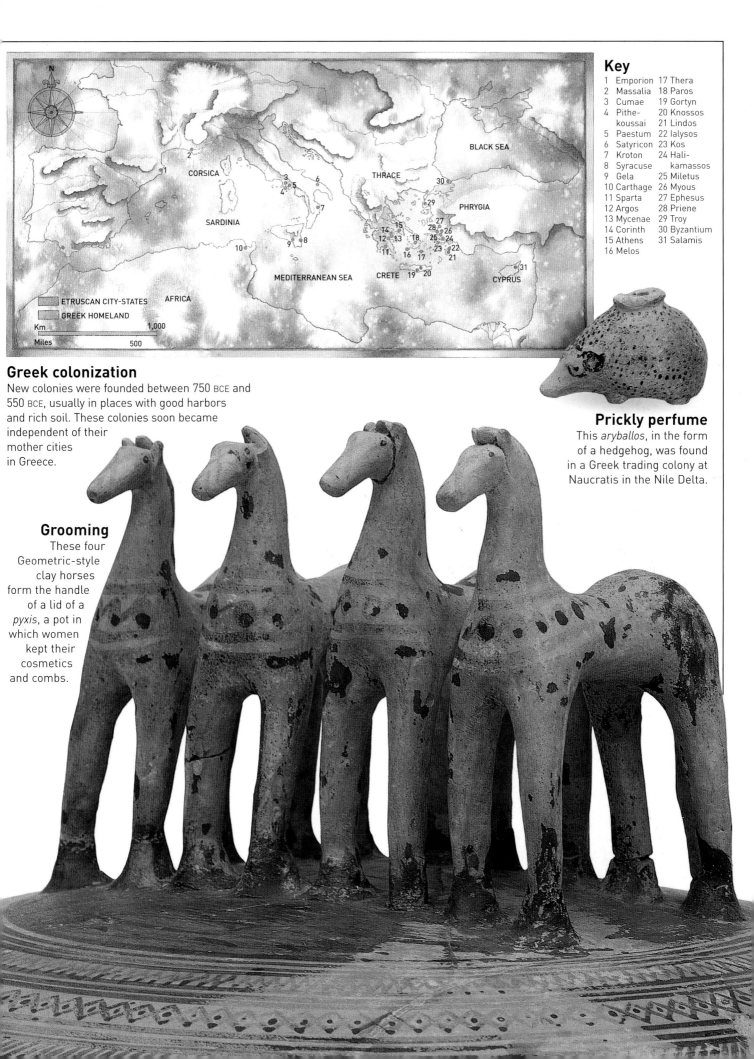

Key

1	Emporion	17	Thera
2	Massalia	18	Paros
3	Cumae	19	Gortyn
4	Pithe-	20	Knossos
	koussai	21	Lindos
5	Paestum	22	Ialysos
6	Satyricon	23	Kos
7	Kroton	24	Hali-
8	Syracuse		kamassos
9	Gela	25	Miletus
10	Carthage	26	Myous
11	Sparta	27	Ephesus
12	Argos	28	Priene
13	Mycenae	29	Troy
14	Corinth	30	Byzantium
15	Athens	31	Salamis
16	Melos		

Greek colonization

New colonies were founded between 750 BCE and 550 BCE, usually in places with good harbors and rich soil. These colonies soon became independent of their mother cities in Greece.

Prickly perfume

This *aryballos*, in the form of a hedgehog, was found in a Greek trading colony at Naucratis in the Nile Delta.

Grooming

These four Geometric-style clay horses form the handle of a lid of a *pyxis*, a pot in which women kept their cosmetics and combs.

City of Athens

The Acropolis
In early times, the Acropolis (high city) was a fortified citadel. Later, it became the most sacred part of Athens.

Sacred statue
The dress shown in this frieze was for a sacred wooden statue of Athena that stood on the Acropolis. The dress is a woven *peplos* (p. 42).

Athens was the most powerful city-state in ancient Greece. It was also the center of arts and learning. Its patron, Athena, was the goddess of wisdom and warfare. In 480 BCE the Persians attacked Athens and destroyed its temples on the Acropolis. After the Greeks finally defeated the Persians (pp. 54–55), Perikles, the leader of Athens (pp. 18–19), began to rebuild the city. The Athenians lived on the land below the Acropolis and many fine buildings have been found by the market place (*agora*). Nearby was Athens' port, the Piraeus. Access to the sea was one of the main reasons for Athens'

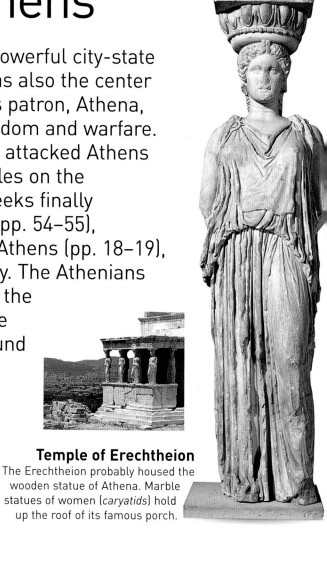

Temple of Erechtheion
The Erechtheion probably housed the wooden statue of Athena. Marble statues of women (*caryatids*) hold up the roof of its famous porch.

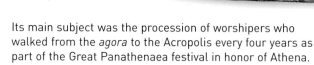

The Parthenon frieze
The marble frieze went around all four sides of the temple and was set up high, on the outside of the central chambers.

Its main subject was the procession of worshipers who walked from the *agora* to the Acropolis every four years as part of the Great Panathenaea festival in honor of Athena.

The Parthenon

The temple of the Parthenon was dedicated to Athena and stood at the highest point of the Acropolis. The Parthenon, which still exists today, was built between 447–432 BCE. Its decorative sculptures were designed by Pheidias.

Golden goddess

Inside the Parthenon stood a huge gold and ivory statue of Athena, the goddess of warfare. In this replica, she wears her *aegis*, a small goatskin cloak fringed with snakes, and a high-crested helmet. On her right hand is a small winged figure of Nike, the goddess of victory.

An Athenian coin showing an owl, the bird of Athena

The Elgin Marbles

Many of the sculptures from the Parthenon were brought to England by Lord Elgin, a British ambassador to the Ottoman court. They can be seen today in the British Museum.

Temporary Elgin Room at the British Museum painted by A. Archer

Young men on horseback take up much of the frieze. Some are trotting gently along and others are galloping with their cloaks flying out behind them.

The background was originally painted, probably a bright blue. The horses used to have bridles made of bronze, but these have not survived.

Politics in Athens

Solon
Solon was a lawgiver who lived in Athens between 640–558 BCE. He passed new laws to prevent poor Athenian farmers from being sold into slavery when they were unable to pay their debts.

In early times, Greece was ruled by rich landlords called tyrants. They were eventually driven out and a new form of government called democracy (rule by the people) was invented in Athens. Political meetings took place at the Assembly on the Pnyx hill, where Athenian citizens could vote and make speeches. At least 6,000 people had to be present for a meeting to take place. There was also a higher Council of 500 members, which met in a round building called the *tholos*. Decisions about the city's defense were made by a group of 10 military commanders, called *strategoi*. These were elected annually and could be reelected many times.

Perikles
Athenian statesman Perikles was elected *strategos* every year from 443–429 BCE. He organized the rebuilding of Athens after its destruction during the Persian wars (490s and 480s BCE).

Boot boy
This bronze figure is of an African boy holding a shoe. Athenian society depended on slaves. Some were employed in wealthy Greek homes, while others worked in the silver mines in Attica. A few slaves received wages and were able to buy back their freedom, but most led lives of drudgery.

Palace of Westminster
The democratic system invented in Athens has inspired many modern governments. The Greek word democracy means "power of the people." However, in Athens, only free male citizens had the right to vote.

Treasury of triumph

The battle of Marathon was a famous victory by the Greeks over the Persians in 490 BCE. This fine marble building was erected at Delphi as a symbol of Athenian triumph. It was both a Treasury, full of objects taken from the Persians, and a religious offering to the god Apollo. It stands by the Sacred Way, which winds up to Apollo's temple. The Treasury illustrates the close links between religion and politics in ancient Greece.

Themistokles

This coin shows Themistokles, an Athenian leader who created the fleet that destroyed the Persians at the battle of Salamis in 480 BCE. (p. 54). He was later banished from Athens.

It is rare to find Greek inscriptions on bronze: usually they were carved in stone

Judgment tablet

This tablet contains a treaty between the cities of Oiantheia and Chaleion. They set up a legal process for solving disputes about land, with penalties if either side broke the treaty.

The carved figures at the top represent Democracy crowning the Athenian People

The decree is carved with the letters in a grid pattern, with no spaces between words—a style called stoichedon

Law against tyranny

The inscription on this *stele* (upright stone slab) outlines the Athenian law against tyranny. Introduced by Eucrates in 336 BCE, this law was one of several decrees passed by the Assembly to protect democracy in Athens.

19

Gods and goddesses

Religion played an important part in Greek life. The Greeks believed that all the gods were descendants of Gaia (the earth) and Uranos (the sky). The gods had supernatural powers, but they also had human qualities: they fell in love, married, quarreled, and had children. Every god or goddess was responsible for a different area of life and people worshiped the gods who would, they believed, then look after them. This worship took the form of building elaborate temples and sanctuaries, holding festivals, making animal sacrifices, and offering them the fruits of the harvest.

Dionysos
Dionysos was the god of wine and the land's fertility.

Zeus
Zeus, the king of the gods, is usually shown as a strong, bearded man. His symbol was a thunderbolt.

Home of the gods
Mount Olympus is the highest mountain in Greece and was believed to be the home of the gods.

Goddess of love
This bronze head of Aphrodite comes from eastern Turkey. It was thought that the goddess was born from sea foam and carried by the Zephyrs (West Winds) to Cyprus.

Beauty and the beast
This mirror case shows Aphrodite (goddess of love and beauty) with her son Eros, shown here as a small, winged boy. She is playing Jacks (pp. 34–35) with Pan, who had the legs and ears of a goat.

Brain child

This vase painting shows the strange birth of Athena, daughter of Zeus and the goddess Metis. Believing that any son born to Metis would be more powerful than his father, Zeus ate Metis. Athena emerged when Zeus ordered the god Hephaistos to cut open his head.

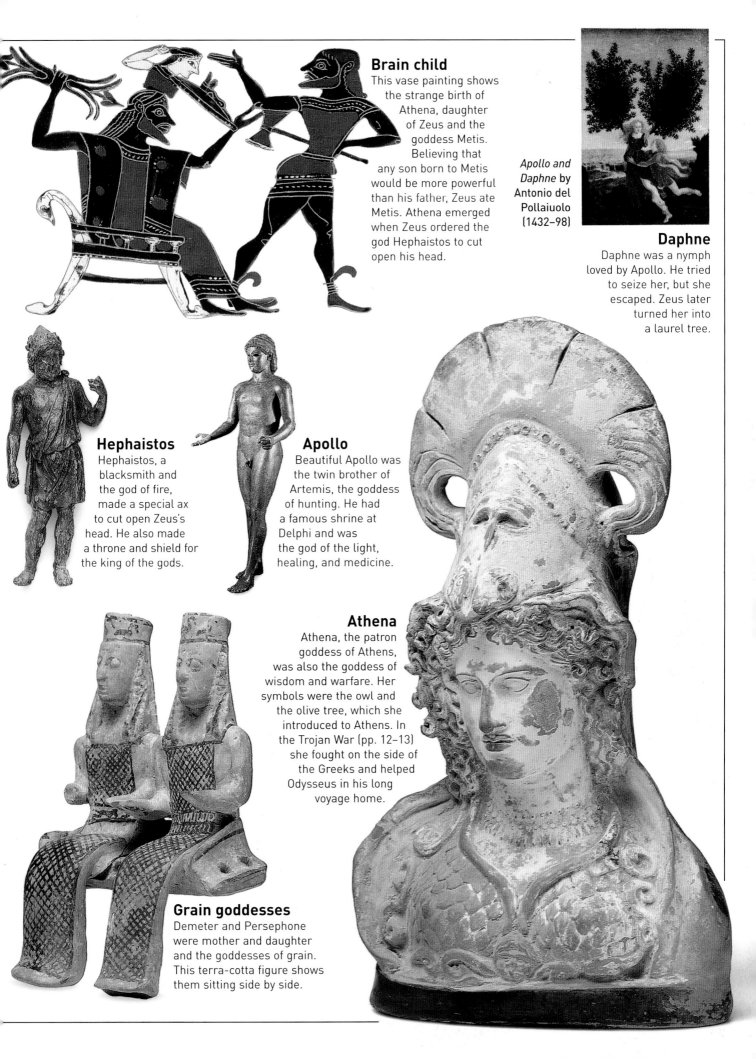

Apollo and Daphne by Antonio del Pollaiuolo (1432–98)

Daphne

Daphne was a nymph loved by Apollo. He tried to seize her, but she escaped. Zeus later turned her into a laurel tree.

Hephaistos

Hephaistos, a blacksmith and the god of fire, made a special ax to cut open Zeus's head. He also made a throne and shield for the king of the gods.

Apollo

Beautiful Apollo was the twin brother of Artemis, the goddess of hunting. He had a famous shrine at Delphi and was the god of the light, healing, and medicine.

Athena

Athena, the patron goddess of Athens, was also the goddess of wisdom and warfare. Her symbols were the owl and the olive tree, which she introduced to Athens. In the Trojan War (pp. 12–13) she fought on the side of the Greeks and helped Odysseus in his long voyage home.

Grain goddesses

Demeter and Persephone were mother and daughter and the goddesses of grain. This terra-cotta figure shows them sitting side by side.

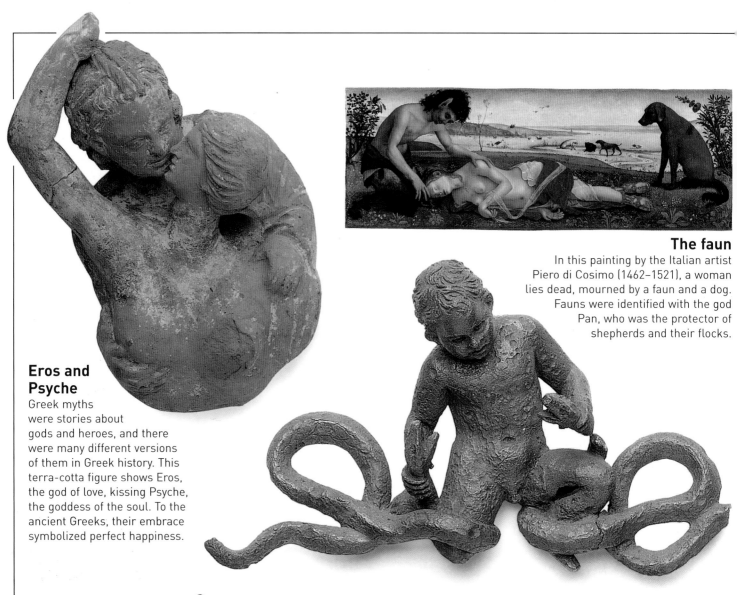

The faun

In this painting by the Italian artist Piero di Cosimo (1462–1521), a woman lies dead, mourned by a faun and a dog. Fauns were identified with the god Pan, who was the protector of shepherds and their flocks.

Eros and Psyche

Greek myths were stories about gods and heroes, and there were many different versions of them in Greek history. This terra-cotta figure shows Eros, the god of love, kissing Psyche, the goddess of the soul. To the ancient Greeks, their embrace symbolized perfect happiness.

Herakles

The great hero Herakles was the son of Zeus by a mortal woman. As a baby, Herakles strangled two snakes with his bare hands. In adult life, he performed 12 famous labors (tasks) for a king named Eurystheus. In the first task, Herakles killed the Nemean lion, and is often shown wearing its skin. The vase painting on the left shows him killing the Stymphalian birds. These birds destroyed crops and wounded people with their poisonous feathers. Herakles scared them with a bronze rattle—given to him by Hephaistos (p. 21)—and then shot them with a sling.

Pegasus
This coin shows the winged horse Pegasus. Pegasus was tamed by Bellerophon, who tried to ride him to heaven. But Pegasus was stung by a gadfly sent by Zeus and threw Bellerophon back down to earth.

Too high!
This bronze is of Icarus, who was given a pair of wings by his father. But he flew too close to the Sun and when the wax holding the wings melted, he fell in the sea and drowned.

The building of the *Argo*
This Roman terra-cotta panel shows Jason (a prince from Thessaly) and the Argonauts (a group of heroes who sailed with him on a ship called the *Argo*). Jason and his crew set sail to find the Golden Fleece that hung on a tree guarded by a snake. The goddess Athena can be seen on the left helping the crew to build the ship.

Lure of the lyre
Orpheus was a poet and a musician, whose singing was famous for its soothing qualities. The magic of Orpheus's music is illustrated in this painting by Dutch painter Roelandt Savery (1576–1639). The wild animals are spellbound by the beautiful sound.

Perseus and Medusa
Medusa was a gorgon whose gaze could turn a person to stone. On this vase painting of 460 BCE, the hero Perseus has just cut off Medusa's head and wrapped it in his bag.

Festivals and oracles

Come dancing
At this festival, a row of people holding hands approach an altar where a sacrifice is blazing. A priestess stands behind the altar with a flat basket used for winnowing grain.

Every Greek city had its own calendar of festivals, during which people made sacrifices to the gods and held games in their honor. The rest of the year, the Greeks worshiped at small altars at home, or in temples dedicated to the gods. One of the greatest temples was that of Apollo at Delphi.

Apollo was a god of prophecy and at Delphi he would reply to questions about the future. A priestess would act as his mouthpiece and make pronouncements that could be interpreted in different ways. These forecasts were known as the oracle.

Holy bull
Bulls were often offered as sacrifices. They were decorated with garlands of plants and ribbons to show that they had been set aside for the gods. Garlanded bulls' heads inspired many of the decorative patterns on Greek temples.

Lucky ruins
This couple is at a Greek temple in ancient Poseidonia (Paestum) in southern Italy. Ancient ruins like these are believed to bring good luck to a new marriage.

Center of the world
The Greeks believed that Delphi was the center of the world. They placed a huge stone there—the *omphalos*, or navel of the world. This version has a network of woolen strands carved upon it, signifying that this was a holy object.

The charioteer

High above the temple of Apollo was a stadium built for games and chariot races in honor of the god. Winning the chariot race was the greatest honor of the games, and the owner of the winning team paid for a statue to celebrate his success. This magnificent bronze statue has eyes inlaid with glass and stone, lips of copper, and a headband decorated with silver. The charioteer still holds the reins of his horses, which have long disappeared.

Temple of Apollo

Delphi was the site of the great temple of Apollo, home of the oracle. The remains of the sanctuary lie on the steep slopes of Mount Parnassus. One road up the slope is still lined with small buildings that used to store gifts offered to the god.

The way to Athena

The Panathenaic Way in Athens led up to Athena's temples on the Acropolis. The road today passes the rebuilt version of a *stoa*, a long, colonnaded building used as a business and meeting place.

Sanctuary of Athena

This circular building stands in the center of the sanctuary of Athena against a background of olive trees. Athena is said to have created the olive tree, and these groves still provide a rich harvest.

Procession of sacrifice

On this wide bowl used for wine, a line of people is on its way to worship the goddess Athena. The goddess is standing behind the altar, where the flames are already rising. Everyone in the procession is carrying objects necessary for worship, such as cakes, wine, musical instruments, and a sacrificial bull.

Temples

Temples were the biggest and most beautiful buildings in ancient Greece. Many were built to celebrate a city's success or to thank a patron god for help during times of war. Temples were made of limestone or marble, with wooden roofs and ceilings. Huge, stone blocks were carried from quarries in ox-drawn carts and carved on site by masons using chisels and hammers. The tall columns were made in cylindrical sections, lifted into place with ropes and pulleys. Decorative friezes and statues added to the grandeur and beauty of the buildings.

Cape Sounion
This fifth-century BCE marble temple to Poseidon (god of the sea) was a landmark for sailors returning home to Athens.

Zeus's temple
The Olympic Games (pp. 44–45) were held every four years at the sanctuary of Olympia. This was also the site of the colossal temple of Zeus built in the fifth century BCE.

Temple of Ceres
Poseidonia (later called Paestum) in southern Italy, was a rich Greek colony and has the best-preserved temples of the Greek world. This one, the temple of Ceres, was later used as a Christian church. For hundreds of years, the site of Paestum was hidden by swamps and undergrowth. This helped to preserve the buildings.

Rosette capital
This huge, marble capital (top of a column) comes from the temple of Artemis at Ephesus in modern Turkey.

Doric
The Doric style is sturdy and its capital is plain. It was often used in the colonies in southern Italy.

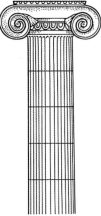

Ionic
The Ionic style is thinner and more elegant. Its capital is decorated with a scroll-like design (a volute).

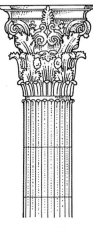

Corinthian
The Corinthian style is often seen on Roman temples. Its ornate capital is decorated with acanthus leaves.

Lion's mouth
Rainwater was often drained from temple roofs through spouts in the form of lions' heads. This one comes from a temple at Priene, south of Ephesus.

Columns and lintels
Most Greek buildings had vertical columns supporting horizontal beams called lintels.

Corinthian capital
This Corinthian capital once decorated a gracious colonnaded building in Asia Minor (modern Turkey). The face is based on a female theatrical mask. The carved acanthus leaves were a favorite motif of Greek artists.

Palmette roof tile
The end of this roof tile is decorated with a palmette shape. It comes from a temple to Apollo at Bassae in southern Greece.

Lotus leaves
This marble fragment is carved with lotus and palmette designs. It comes from the famous temple of the Erechtheion in Athens (pp. 16–17). The roof of the south porch of the building is supported by columns in the form of standing women with baskets on their heads. Perikles ordered the construction of the Erechtheion to beautify the city of Athens.

At home

The Greeks liked their homes to be private. Outer windows were small and set high in the walls, which were made out of sun-dried mud bricks. This farmhouse is a fairly simple building. Townhouses had more rooms and were probably more luxurious. All the rooms led off a central courtyard or garden. A statue of the god Hermes (a *herm*) was placed in the porch to prevent evil spirits from entering.

Terra-cotta figurine shows a woman grinding grain to make bread

Wooden doors
Doors were precious objects, because wood was expensive in Greece.

Rain cat
Rainwater flowed from gutters through spouts like this one in the form of a lion's head.

Ladder to upper story

Altar where sacrifices were offered to the gods

The women's quarters *(gynaeceum)* housed the weaving looms, babies' cradles, and couches

Hearth for cooking and to provide burning charcoal for portable braziers

The dining room *(andron)* where guests were entertained

On the tiles

Sometimes, in wealthy houses, the ends of the terra-cotta roof tiles were decorated with human and animal faces. This gorgon head has tight curls and a protruding tongue.

Sitting pretty

In this vase painting, a young woman is sitting on a chair in her house. This elegant shape of chair is often seen on vases.

Couches

Because Greek couches were made mainly of wood, none have survived. This bronze decoration was once attached to a couch near the head rest.

Roof made of clay tiles

Walls made of mud bricks, sometimes plastered over

Window openings without glass but with wooden shutters

Wooden door with bronze fittings

Stone foundations were often stolen by later builders

Porch pillars made from fallen or cut-down trees on the farm land

In the country, a stone wall usually surrounded the property

Women

The lives of women in ancient Greece were fairly restricted. They were very much under the control of their husbands, fathers, or brothers, and rarely took part in public life. Girls married young, at the age of 13 or 14. The main purpose of marriage was to have children, and a woman's status was greatly improved if she gave birth to a boy (pp. 32–33). Although legally they had very little freedom, some women could make important decisions about family life. Their spinning and weaving work also made an important contribution to the household.

Whorl

Spindle
Wool was spun into yarn with a spindle. At one end is a weight, known as a spindle whorl. The spindle twirls around and spins the wool fiber into thread.

Greek Woman by British artist Sir Lawrence Alma-Tadema

Homemakers
Greek girls did not go to school (pp. 32–33). Instead they were taught how to look after the home. Some wealthy women did, however, learn to read and write.

Spinning tools
This woman is using both a spindle and a distaff (a shaft with a spike at one end and a handle at the other).

Well women
In Athens, women and slave girls went to fill their water pots at public fountains, since few houses had their own private wells. The women waited in turn with their water pots balanced on their heads. This was a good opportunity to meet with friends and chat.

This *epinetron* shows women spinning and weaving

Thigh protector

To prepare the wool for spinning, a woman fitted an instrument called an *epinetron* over her knee. She then rolled the wool across the surface of it and drew it out, creating thin skeins of wool.

Sappho

The poet Sappho lived on the island of Lesbos in the late seventh century BCE. Her poems give a rare glimpse of the lives and feelings of many women at the time.

Beauty aid

Wealthy women owned many beauty aids. This bronze mirror, which would have been highly polished when new, has a stand in the form of a goddess holding a dove. Two little cupid figures fly on either side of her. Large numbers of caskets, combs, and perfume bottles have also been found at various sites.

The little lamps burning on the tables in front of the diners were used to light darkened rooms

Entertainers

Respectable women were expected to stay at home, keeping house and supervising the slaves. Only women called *hetairai* were allowed to attend the *symposia* (banquets, pp. 36–37). Groups of *hetairai* are often seen on vases playing the pipes, dancing, and entertaining the male guests.

Growing up in Greece

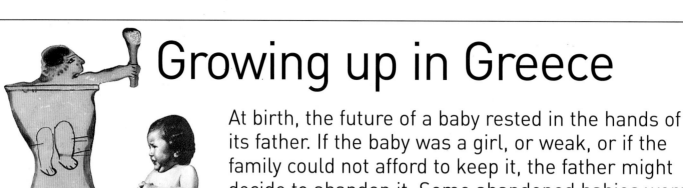

Potty training
This vase painting shows a little boy sitting in a potty, which also seems to double as a high chair.

Modern baby sitting on an ancient potty

At birth, the future of a baby rested in the hands of its father. If the baby was a girl, or weak, or if the family could not afford to keep it, the father might decide to abandon it. Some abandoned babies were saved by other families and brought up as slaves. However, once a baby had been accepted by its family, he or she was treated kindly. Boys went to school at the age of seven. Girls stayed at home. At the age of 12 or 13, children were regarded as young adults and would dedicate their toys to the god Apollo and the goddess Artemis to show that they had reached the end of childhood.

A bowl on a stand used in a marriage ceremony

Faster! Faster!
This painting from a wine pitcher shows two young boys pulling their friend in a go-cart. At the wine festival in Athens, pitchers were given as presents to boys when they reached the age of three to show that babyhood was over.

Girl's grave
This dignified terra-cotta doll, sitting in a high-backed chair, was found in the tomb of a little girl. The doll probably represents the woman the girl might have become in adult life.

A pair of boots, a sign of adulthood

Education

At school, boys learned reading, writing, and arithmetic from a teacher called a *grammatistes*. Music was taught by a teacher known as a *kitharistes*. Boys also had to study poetry and the art of debating. Older boys might be taught by teachers called sophists, who traveled from town to town and often taught their students in a *gymnasium,* or training ground. Although girls did not go to school, some girls from wealthy families had private tutors.

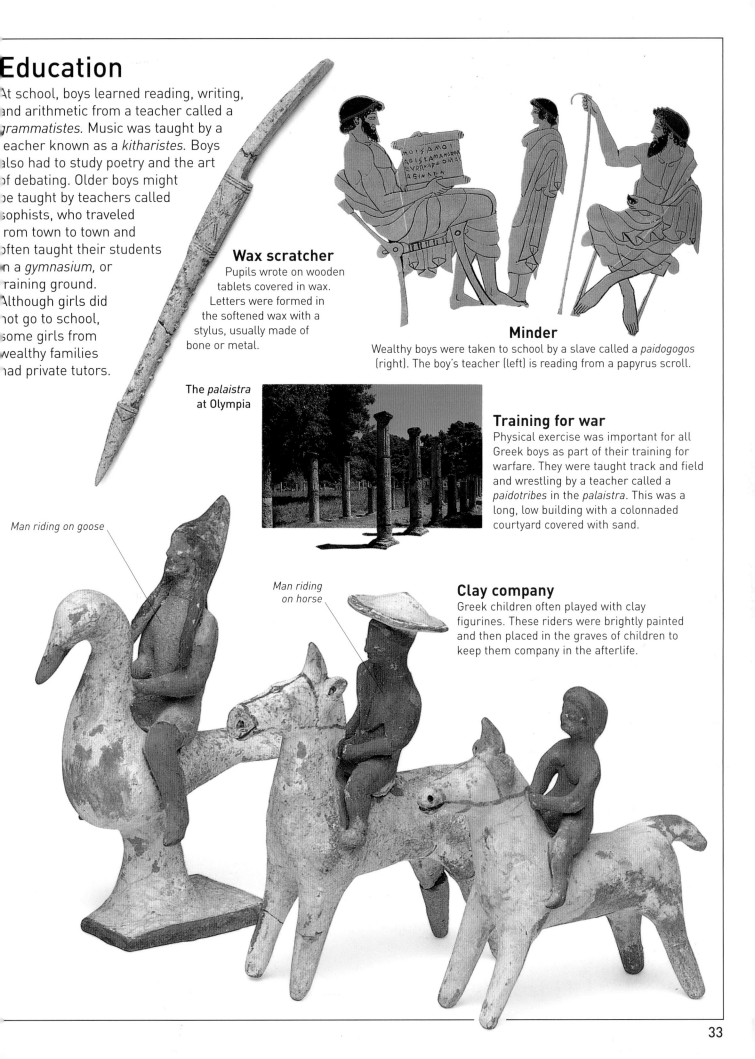

Wax scratcher
Pupils wrote on wooden tablets covered in wax. Letters were formed in the softened wax with a stylus, usually made of bone or metal.

The *palaistra* at Olympia

Minder
Wealthy boys were taken to school by a slave called a *paidogogos* (right). The boy's teacher (left) is reading from a papyrus scroll.

Training for war
Physical exercise was important for all Greek boys as part of their training for warfare. They were taught track and field and wrestling by a teacher called a *paidotribes* in the *palaistra*. This was a long, low building with a colonnaded courtyard covered with sand.

Man riding on goose

Man riding on horse

Clay company
Greek children often played with clay figurines. These riders were brightly painted and then placed in the graves of children to keep them company in the afterlife.

Fun and games

Rich Greeks spent their leisure time giving dinner parties, visiting the *gymnasium*, and playing all kinds of games. The Greeks loved singing and played a variety of musical instruments including the harp, the lyre, and the panpipes. Unfortunately, almost no written music has survived from ancient Greece, although there are many vase paintings showing Greek women dancing. Greek men did not dance, but they liked to be entertained by dancers at drinking parties (pp. 36–37). Poor Greeks, such as farmers and slaves, had very little spare time for leisure activities.

Dancing girl
This slave girl is probably an entertainer at a party. She is playing the castanets.

Clash of cymbals
Few musical instruments have survived, although they are often seen on vase paintings. These cymbals are inscribed with their owner's name.

Jacks

Tuneful trio
This vase painting shows three people playing their musical instruments. The seated woman is the Muse Terpsichore. Muses were minor goddesses who looked after the arts. The man on the right is Musaios, a legendary musician.

Large lyre
The kithara, which this woman is playing, is a larger, wooden version of the lyre. She is plucking the strings with a plectrum, similar to those used by guitarists today. The kithara was usually played by professional musicians.

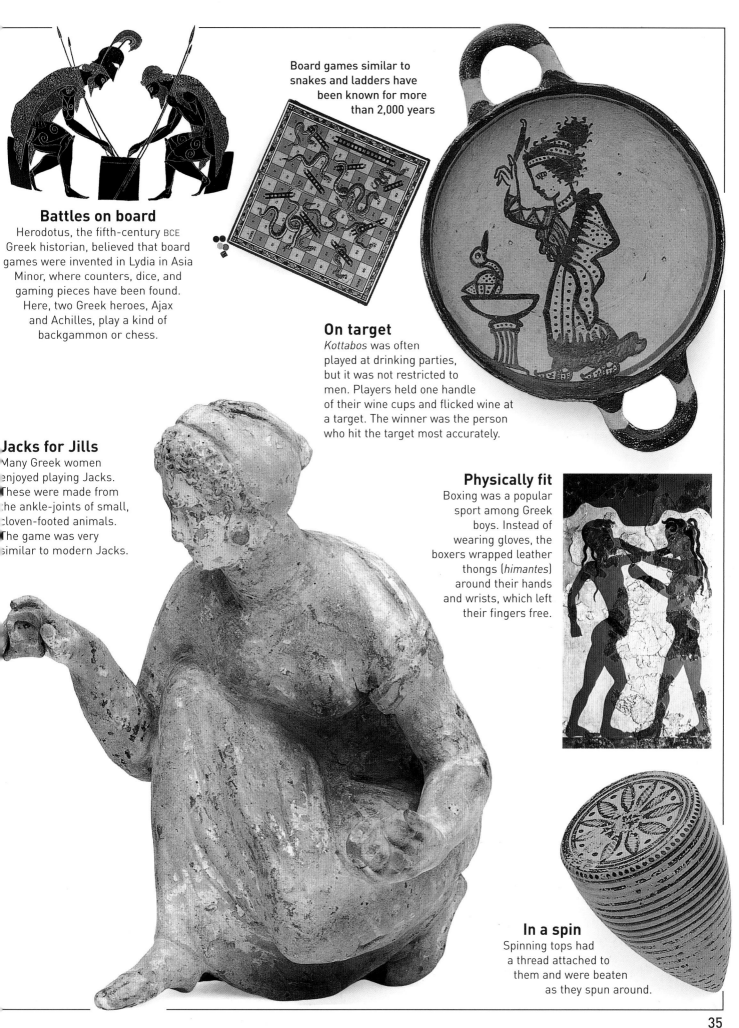

Battles on board

Herodotus, the fifth-century BCE Greek historian, believed that board games were invented in Lydia in Asia Minor, where counters, dice, and gaming pieces have been found. Here, two Greek heroes, Ajax and Achilles, play a kind of backgammon or chess.

Board games similar to snakes and ladders have been known for more than 2,000 years

On target

Kottabos was often played at drinking parties, but it was not restricted to men. Players held one handle of their wine cups and flicked wine at a target. The winner was the person who hit the target most accurately.

Jacks for Jills

Many Greek women enjoyed playing Jacks. These were made from the ankle-joints of small, cloven-footed animals. The game was very similar to modern Jacks.

Physically fit

Boxing was a popular sport among Greek boys. Instead of wearing gloves, the boxers wrapped leather thongs (*himantes*) around their hands and wrists, which left their fingers free.

In a spin

Spinning tops had a thread attached to them and were beaten as they spun around.

35

Wining and dining

Diver's tomb
This banqueting scene is painted on a tomb wall at Paestum, a Greek colony in Italy. Young men recline on couches, while slaves serve them food and wine.

Greek men often held drinking parties (*symposia*) for their male friends. *Symposia* took place at home in the dining room (*andron*). All respectable women were excluded, but slave girls called *hetairai* would entertain the men with dancing, flute playing, and acrobatic displays (p. 31). The guests wore garlands and perfume and began their evening with special songs to the gods. Topics of discussion might include politics or philosophy. Eventually, the banqueters would fall asleep on couches.

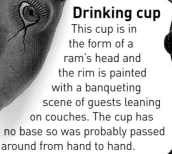

Drinking cup
This cup is in the form of a ram's head and the rim is painted with a banqueting scene of guests leaning on couches. The cup has no base so was probably passed around from hand to hand.

Bowls of olives both green and black, would have been offered at a *symposion*, possibly as an appetizer

Wine vessels
Wine was a favorite drink of the Greeks and was nearly always diluted with water. Bread dipped in wine and eaten with a few figs was a typical Greek breakfast. Wine containers were made of clay or bronze. The large vessel on the far left was used to mix water and wine. A slave would ladle the mixture into the pitcher, then fill his master's cup.

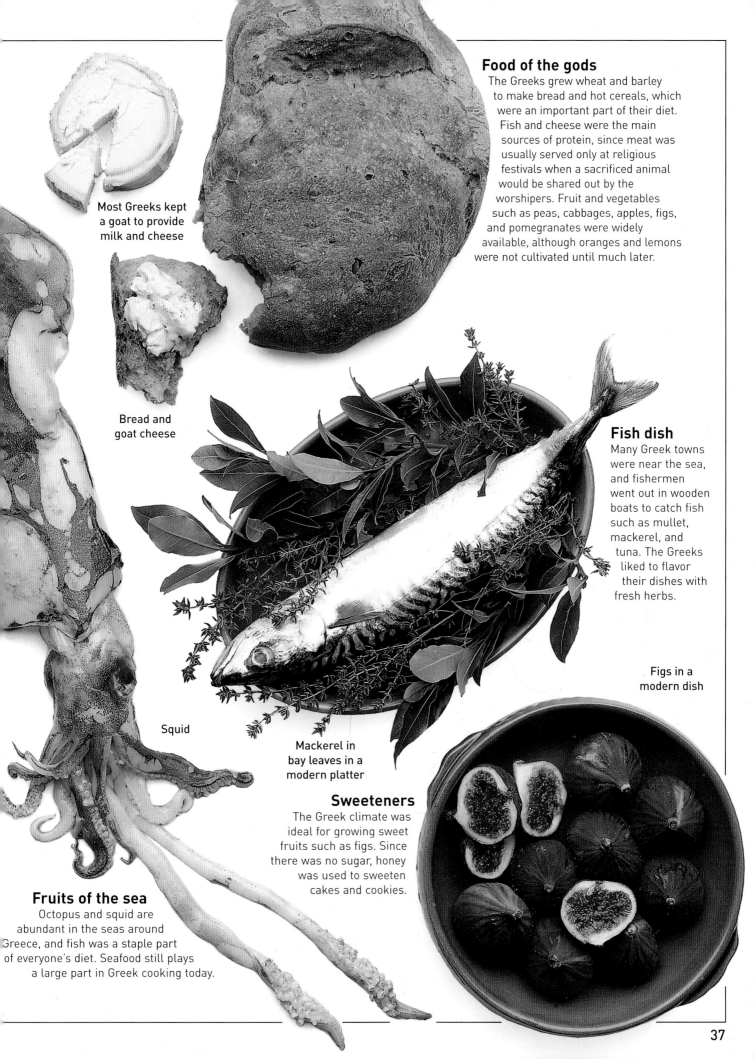

Food of the gods

The Greeks grew wheat and barley to make bread and hot cereals, which were an important part of their diet. Fish and cheese were the main sources of protein, since meat was usually served only at religious festivals when a sacrificed animal would be shared out by the worshipers. Fruit and vegetables such as peas, cabbages, apples, figs, and pomegranates were widely available, although oranges and lemons were not cultivated until much later.

Most Greeks kept a goat to provide milk and cheese

Bread and goat cheese

Fish dish

Many Greek towns were near the sea, and fishermen went out in wooden boats to catch fish such as mullet, mackerel, and tuna. The Greeks liked to flavor their dishes with fresh herbs.

Figs in a modern dish

Squid

Mackerel in bay leaves in a modern platter

Sweeteners

The Greek climate was ideal for growing sweet fruits such as figs. Since there was no sugar, honey was used to sweeten cakes and cookies.

Fruits of the sea

Octopus and squid are abundant in the seas around Greece, and fish was a staple part of everyone's diet. Seafood still plays a large part in Greek cooking today.

A day out

Greek theaters were spectacular buildings. At sacred sites, such as Delphi and Epidauros, people flocked to see dramas in honor of the gods. In the sixth century BCE, drama competitions took place during the spring festival of the wine god Dionysos. By the fifth century BCE, both tragedies and comedies were being performed, many of which survive today. The flat central *orchestra* was used for dancing and singing, often performed by a group of actors called the chorus, who commented on the play's action. All the actors were men, who wore masks. Women were probably not allowed to go to the theater at all.

Euripides
Euripides, an Athenian playwright in the fifth century BCE, wrote tragedies about serious subjects, such as the horrors of war.

Tired out
This small terracotta figure shows a comic actor dressed as a weary old woman. He wears a mask with a wrinkled face and crinkly hair.

Bird's-eye view
From high up in the back row at Epidauros you can get a clear view of the performance.

Epidauros
The theater at Epidauros could seat 14,000 spectators. This ground-level view gives an idea of what it was like to be an actor going into the performing area. The carefully curved auditorium (*theatron*) is a huge, semicircular bowl cut into the surface of the hillside. Its shape is not just designed for excellent viewing; it also captures sound so that actors speaking in the *orchestra* can be heard by people in the back row.

Sophokles

This print decorates a 19th-century text of the plays of Sophokles, who wrote about royal or legendary families and their tragic lives. His stories of King Oedipus or Electra, daughter of Agamemnon, still grip modern audiences.

Aeschylus

Here, modern actors perform *The Oresteia* by playwright Aeschylus. It describes how Orestes set out to avenge the death of his father, Agamemnon.

The very elaborate hat is a sign that this bearded man's wealth was not acquired honestly

The muse holds a mask portraying a young woman, one of the characters in Greek comedy from the fourth century BCE

Souvenirs

Statuettes in terra-cotta, originally painted in bright colors, were probably souvenirs of theater visits. Sets of the entire casts of plays have been found in graves. The graceful female figure is probably a muse, one of the nine guardians of the arts in Greek mythology.

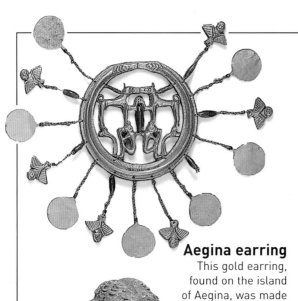

Greek beauty

Beauty and cleanliness were very important to the ancient Greeks. In sculpture and on vases, both men and women can be seen posing gracefully in elegant, draped garments (pp. 42–43). Young men had to keep themselves in shape to be good soldiers and athletes. Nudity was considered normal for young men, who competed naked in athletic festivals (pp. 44–45). Women wore light, loose clothes made of finely spun wool and they perfumed their hair with oils. Wealthy women wore ornate jewelry, usually in gold and silver.

Aegina earring
This gold earring, found on the island of Aegina, was made in Minoan times (pp. 8–9). It shows two dogs standing on monkeys' heads enclosed by a snake.

Grave relief
On this grave relief, a slave is shown handing a bracelet to a woman, quite possibly the dead person herself.

Follower of fashion
This terra-cotta figurine shows a fashionable Greek woman wearing a tunic and cloak (pp. 42–43) and holding a fan. Clothes were often brightly colored, as can be seen from the traces of paint on the statuette. Hairstyles were elaborate, as shown on this woman, who is wearing a head decoration.

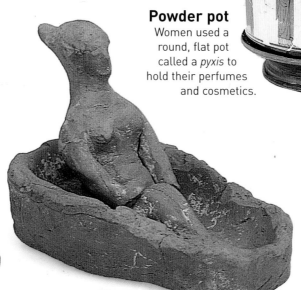

Powder pot
Women used a round, flat pot called a *pyxis* to hold their perfumes and cosmetics.

Bathtime
At the foot of this bathtub was a hollow where the water was deeper so that the woman could splash it backward over her body.

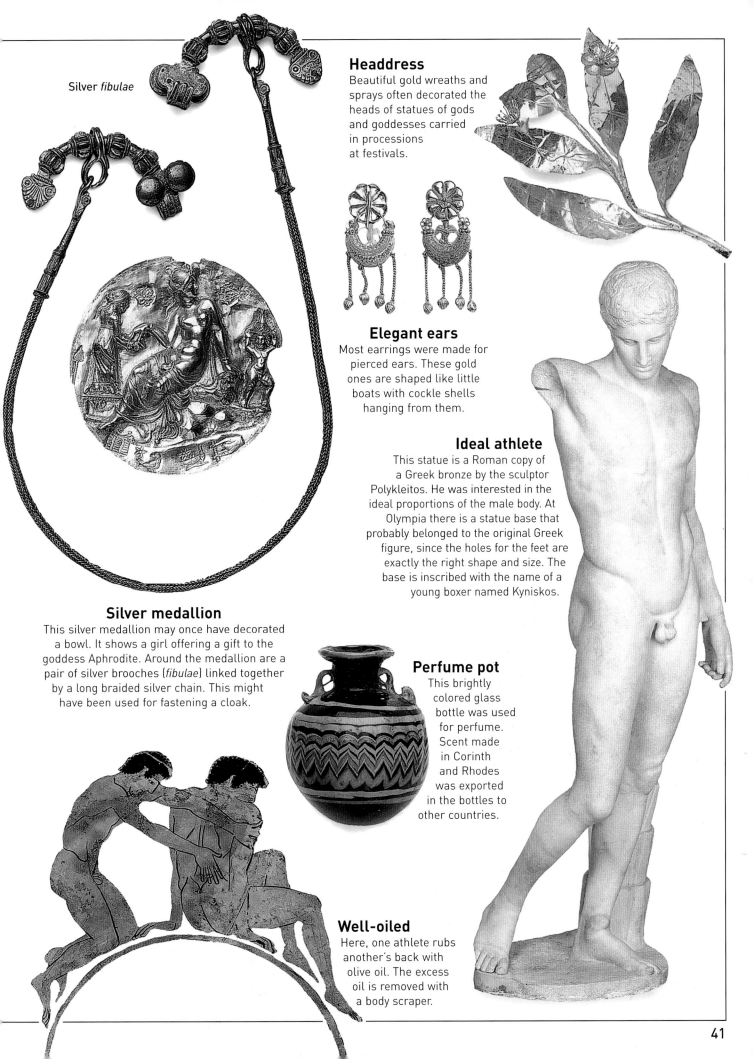

Silver *fibulae*

Headdress
Beautiful gold wreaths and sprays often decorated the heads of statues of gods and goddesses carried in processions at festivals.

Elegant ears
Most earrings were made for pierced ears. These gold ones are shaped like little boats with cockle shells hanging from them.

Ideal athlete
This statue is a Roman copy of a Greek bronze by the sculptor Polykleitos. He was interested in the ideal proportions of the male body. At Olympia there is a statue base that probably belonged to the original Greek figure, since the holes for the feet are exactly the right shape and size. The base is inscribed with the name of a young boxer named Kyniskos.

Silver medallion
This silver medallion may once have decorated a bowl. It shows a girl offering a gift to the goddess Aphrodite. Around the medallion are a pair of silver brooches (*fibulae*) linked together by a long braided silver chain. This might have been used for fastening a cloak.

Perfume pot
This brightly colored glass bottle was used for perfume. Scent made in Corinth and Rhodes was exported in the bottles to other countries.

Well-oiled
Here, one athlete rubs another's back with olive oil. The excess oil is removed with a body scraper.

Getting dressed

Greek clothes were usually made from very fine wool or linen. Very wealthy people bought expensive silks from the east. Bright colors were popular, especially among women. Purple dyes came from sea snails and insect larvae. Other dyes were made from plants. The shapes of clothes were much the same for men and women and hardly changed over hundreds of years. The basic dress was a straight tunic fastened at the shoulder with pins and worn under a cloak.

Lady Hamilton
Sir William Hamilton, British Ambassador to Naples in the late 18th century, collected Greek antiquities. His wife, Emma, often dressed in Greek costume.

Hair dressing
Greek women had long hair, which they piled up at the back of the head and held in place with a net and ribbons. Ornate hair decorations were worn on special occasions.

Ready to wear
The *chiton* was said to have been invented in the region of Ionia. It was made from a single rectangle of cloth, cut into two, and fastened at intervals from the neck to the elbows. It was then gathered at the waist with a belt. Another earlier kind of *chiton*, sometimes called a *peplos*, originated in mainland Greece. It was secured with big pins on the shoulders and did not have sleeves.

Chiton

Chiton

Wrap up
Greek underwear was not fitted, but was wrapped around the body. This woman is pulling her *chiton* over her head.

Greek fantasy
Sir Lawrence Alma-Tadema (pp. 30–31) often chose Greek subjects for his paintings. The clothing and architecture are based more on his imagination than on historical fact.

Chiton

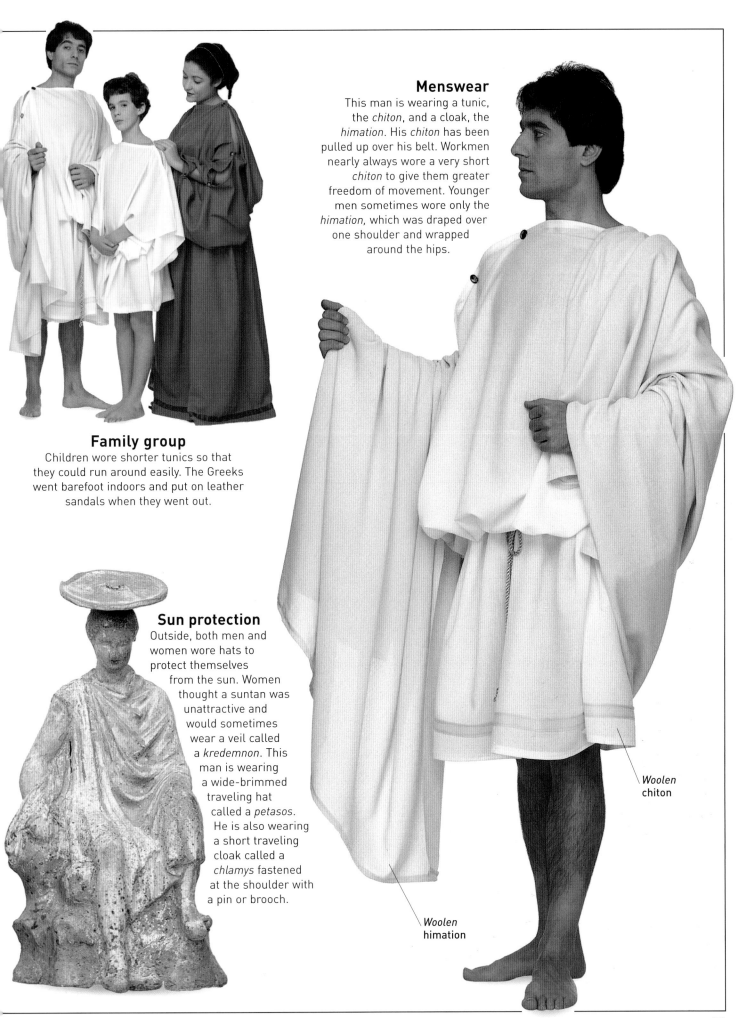

Menswear

This man is wearing a tunic, the *chiton*, and a cloak, the *himation*. His *chiton* has been pulled up over his belt. Workmen nearly always wore a very short *chiton* to give them greater freedom of movement. Younger men sometimes wore only the *himation*, which was draped over one shoulder and wrapped around the hips.

Family group

Children wore shorter tunics so that they could run around easily. The Greeks went barefoot indoors and put on leather sandals when they went out.

Sun protection

Outside, both men and women wore hats to protect themselves from the sun. Women thought a suntan was unattractive and would sometimes wear a veil called a *kredemnon*. This man is wearing a wide-brimmed traveling hat called a *petasos*. He is also wearing a short traveling cloak called a *chlamys* fastened at the shoulder with a pin or brooch.

Woolen chiton

Woolen himation

The Greek games

Champions
This fourth-century BCE statue shows how difficult it was to race in ancient Greece. The jockey rides bareback with no stirrups.

Greek men took part in sporting activities as part of their training for warfare and as a way of honoring the gods. Four major athletics festivals were held in ancient Greece. Of these, the most important was the Olympic Games, held every four years in honor of Zeus at Olympia. Wars were suspended to allow safe travel to and from Olympia and success in the games brought great honor. The four-yearly Panathenaic Games were held in Athens in honor of Athena. Discipline in sports was strict and breaking the rules was punished severely.

Training time
Wrestling was one of the most dangerous sports. Biting or gouging out eyes was strictly forbidden. The man on the left is in a racing start position and the man on the right is testing his javelin.

Prize pots
This boxing scene (336 BCE) was painted on a special kind of olive oil pot given as a prize to victorious athletes at the festival of Athena. Known as Panathenaic vases, they always had a painting of Athena on one side and the sporting event on the other.

The Delphi stadium
The stadium at Delphi could hold up to 7,000 spectators. The stone starting grooves on the track can still be seen, as well as many of the seats that were cut into the mountain side.

The Olympic spirit
Many artists have been inspired by the spirit of the Olympic Games. This 19th-century German illustration shows naked athletes exercising.

The pentathlon
These athletes are taking part in the pentathlon, an event that included discus and javelin throwing, running, jumping, and wrestling.

Dedicated discus
This bronze discus was made in the sixth century BCE. The inscription says that it was thrown by an athlete named Exoidas, who won a contest with it. He dedicated the discus to Castor and Pollux, the twin sons of Zeus. Pollux was a champion discus thrower.

The discus thrower
This famous marble statue of a discus thrower is a copy of a Greek bronze original.

Torchlight
This runner is carrying an Olympic flame. In Athens, relay races with torches took place after dark. The winners lit a fire on the altars of Zeus or Athena.

Longer jumps
Long-jump athletes used stone or lead jumping weights. This Roman example had grooves for a firm grip. Holding the weights, the athletes would throw their arms backward to help them take off.

Modern games
The Olympic tradition continues today. The Olympics are held every four years and are divided between the winter and summer. Cities compete globally to host the event, building new stadia and facilities to accommodate the competitors, media, and tourists.

The first modern Olympics
The first modern Olympics were held in 1896 in Athens. They were organized by Pierre de Coubertin, a French aristocrat.

Wisdom and beauty

The ancient Greeks were pioneers in science and philosophy (which means the "love of wisdom"). Early thinkers were interested in the physical world. Democritus believed the universe was made up of atoms, and Heroclitus thought that the universe was made from fire. Philosophy and the arts were part of religion, too. Religious hymns celebrated the meaning and mystery of life and explained the origin of the gods. The Greeks made beautiful objects, both as offerings to the gods and for their own use. Music, dance, sculpture, painting, and pottery all thrived in ancient Greece.

Royal pupil
Here, the philosopher Aristotle is tutoring the young prince Alexander of Macedon (pp. 62–63).

Pipes
This sycamore pipe is one of a pair; Greeks played sets of double pipes. Originally there would have been a reed in the mouthpiece.

Vase painter
Exekias, a Greek potter and vase painter, produced many beautiful pieces of work. This exquisitely painted drinking cup shows the god Dionysos reclining in a boat, with his special plant, the vine, twining around the mast. The dolphins may be pirates who tried to capture him and who were turned into sea creatures.

Pythagoras holding the cosmos

Lyre
This stringed instrument was originally made from an empty tortoise shell. Its strings could be tightened to produce a range of notes.

The key to the cosmos
Pythagoras (c. 580–500 BCE), who came from the island of Samos, was the leader of a group of religious thinkers in southern Italy. They believed that the world (cosmos) was based on mathematical patterns.

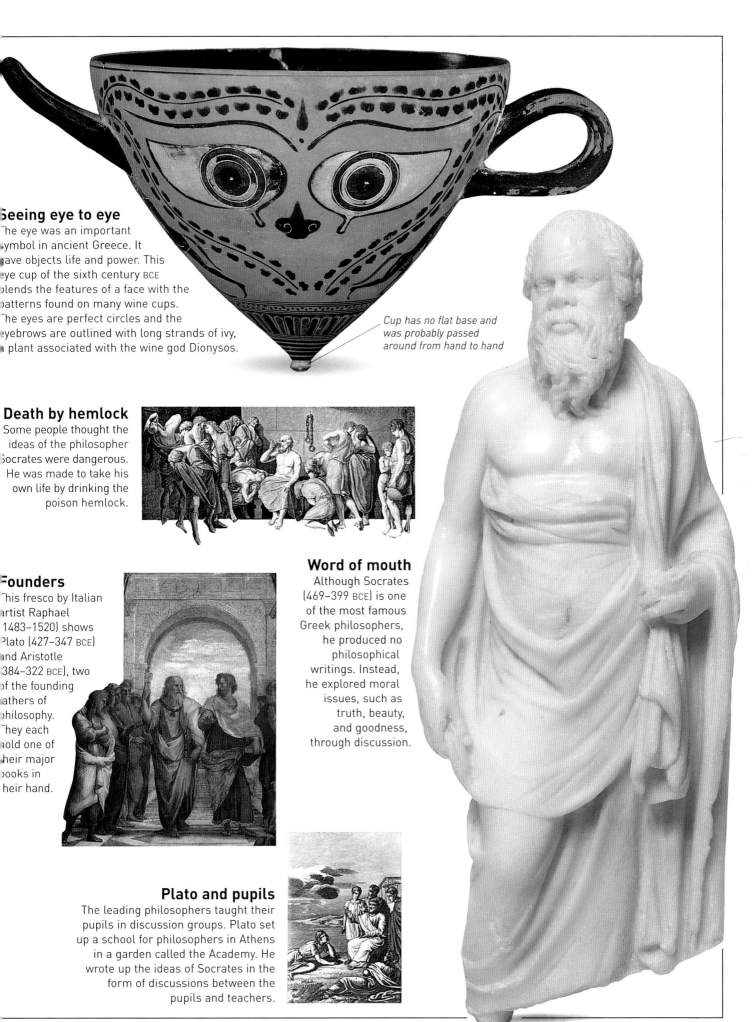

Seeing eye to eye

The eye was an important symbol in ancient Greece. It gave objects life and power. This eye cup of the sixth century BCE blends the features of a face with the patterns found on many wine cups. The eyes are perfect circles and the eyebrows are outlined with long strands of ivy, a plant associated with the wine god Dionysos.

Cup has no flat base and was probably passed around from hand to hand

Death by hemlock

Some people thought the ideas of the philosopher Socrates were dangerous. He was made to take his own life by drinking the poison hemlock.

Founders

This fresco by Italian artist Raphael (1483–1520) shows Plato (427–347 BCE) and Aristotle (384–322 BCE), two of the founding fathers of philosophy. They each hold one of their major books in their hand.

Word of mouth

Although Socrates (469–399 BCE) is one of the most famous Greek philosophers, he produced no philosophical writings. Instead, he explored moral issues, such as truth, beauty, and goodness, through discussion.

Plato and pupils

The leading philosophers taught their pupils in discussion groups. Plato set up a school for philosophers in Athens in a garden called the Academy. He wrote up the ideas of Socrates in the form of discussions between the pupils and teachers.

Vases and vessels

The best Greek pottery was made in Athens, where the local clay fired to a beautiful reddish-brown color. Athenian potters worked in an area called the *Kerameikos*, where they produced pottery for home and export. Geometric patterns were in fashion between 1000–700 BCE. By 720 BCE, Oriental motifs had become popular. In the black-figure technique of the sixth century BCE, black silhouette figures were painted on the reddish clay background. Soon after 500 BCE, the red-figure technique took over, in which figures were left unpainted to stand out against a black background.

Black-figure vase

Drink up!
Drinking cups in the form of animal heads were very fashionable. This angry-looking griffin *rhyton* is a good example.

Trefoil top

First sip
This miniature wine pitcher is called a *chous*. It would have been filled with wine and given to a little boy as a special present during the festival of Dionysos, the god of wine.

What a boar!
The stories of Herakles (p. 22) inspired artists. Here, he holds the Erymanthian boar above King Eurystheus.

The purplish-red color is a mixture of the black clay solution and red iron oxide

Water pot
This 19th-century cartoon shows Sir William Hamilton (p. 42) caricatured as a water pot (*hydria*).

Vase vault
This engraving shows Sir William at a tomb in Italy. The skeleton is surrounded by vases from Athens.

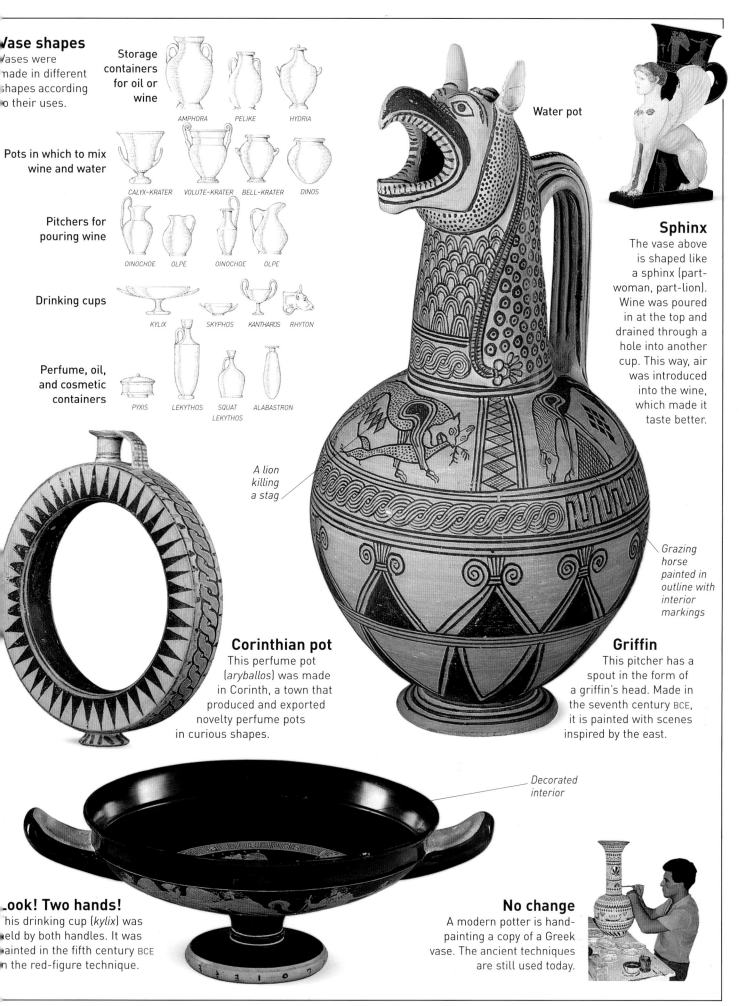

Vase shapes

Vases were made in different shapes according to their uses.

Storage containers for oil or wine

AMPHORA   PELIKE   HYDRIA

Pots in which to mix wine and water

CALYX-KRATER   VOLUTE-KRATER   BELL-KRATER   DINOS

Pitchers for pouring wine

OINOCHOE   OLPE   OINOCHOE   OLPE

Drinking cups

KYLIX   SKYPHOS   KANTHAROS   RHYTON

Perfume, oil, and cosmetic containers

PYXIS   LEKYTHOS   SQUAT LEKYTHOS   ALABASTRON

Water pot

A lion killing a stag

Sphinx

The vase above is shaped like a sphinx (part-woman, part-lion). Wine was poured in at the top and drained through a hole into another cup. This way, air was introduced into the wine, which made it taste better.

Grazing horse painted in outline with interior markings

Corinthian pot

This perfume pot (*aryballos*) was made in Corinth, a town that produced and exported novelty perfume pots in curious shapes.

Griffin

This pitcher has a spout in the form of a griffin's head. Made in the seventh century BCE, it is painted with scenes inspired by the east.

Decorated interior

Look! Two hands!

This drinking cup (*kylix*) was held by both handles. It was painted in the fifth century BCE in the red-figure technique.

No change

A modern potter is hand-painting a copy of a Greek vase. The ancient techniques are still used today.

Farming and fishing

Life for Greek farmers was difficult because much of the soil was poor. Wooden plows, pulled by oxen, were often tipped with iron to make them sharper. Farmers prayed to Zeus and Demeter, goddess of grain, for a good harvest.

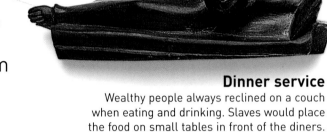

Dinner service
Wealthy people always reclined on a couch when eating and drinking. Slaves would place the food on small tables in front of the diners.

Grapes were grown for wine, which was the most popular Greek drink. Most people lived near the sea and fishermen caught a variety of fish using bronze fish hooks. The wealthy hunted deer and boar, but poorer people ate meat only on special occasions.

Tending sheep
A shepherd's work today is much as it was in ancient times.

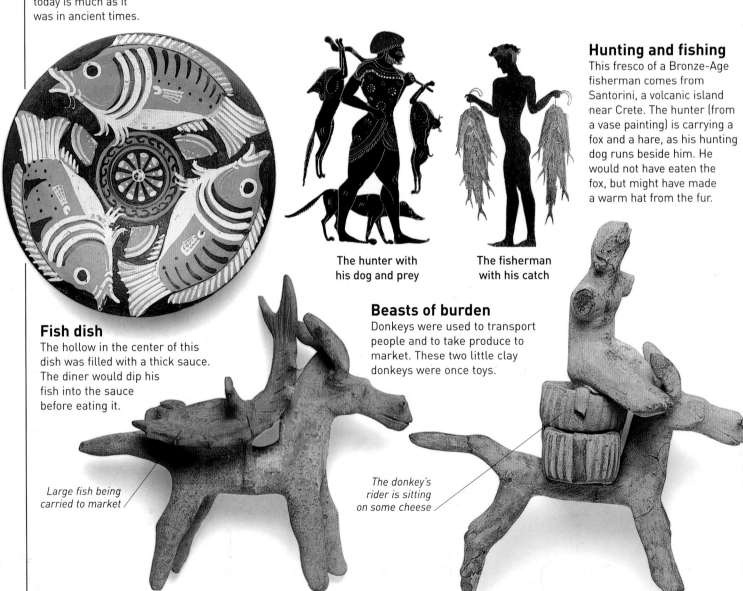

Hunting and fishing
This fresco of a Bronze-Age fisherman comes from Santorini, a volcanic island near Crete. The hunter (from a vase painting) is carrying a fox and a hare, as his hunting dog runs beside him. He would not have eaten the fox, but might have made a warm hat from the fur.

The hunter with his dog and prey

The fisherman with his catch

Fish dish
The hollow in the center of this dish was filled with a thick sauce. The diner would dip his fish into the sauce before eating it.

Large fish being carried to market

Beasts of burden
Donkeys were used to transport people and to take produce to market. These two little clay donkeys were once toys.

The donkey's rider is sitting on some cheese

Duck's head decorates the end of the strainer

Swimming in oil
This little dolphin skimming over the waves was used to store olive oil. Dolphins were common around the coasts of Greece.

Fine wine
Wine was enjoyed at all times of the day. Because it was thick, it needed to be strained and was usually diluted with water. There were many utensils for wine. This strainer is made of bronze.

Olive harvest
Olive trees thrive in Greece. This vase shows four farmers harvesting olives. One is sitting in the tree, two are shaking the branches, and another is gathering the fallen olives.

Olive oil
Olive oil was used in cooking, washing, and lighting.

Dregs collected in the bottom of the strainer

Fossilized snail on egg

Goat for all seasons
Goats provided milk and cheese, and their skins were made into warm winter clothes. This bronze goat was made in about 500 BCE.

Egg cup
These hen's eggs, found in a tomb on the island of Rhodes, are more than 2,000 years old. Many households kept hens, and eggs were a staple food. Funeral offerings of eggs were common in Greek graves. They were probably a symbol of life after death.

Crafts, travel, and trade

Craftsmen such as stone carvers, metalworkers, and jewelers flourished in the cities of ancient Greece. They sold their wares at the *agora*, or marketplace. Farmers brought their produce to market on carts pulled by donkeys. The roads were poor and most people did not travel far from home. Long journeys were made by boat to avoid the mountains. There was a great deal of trade between the city-states and the Greek colonies, as well as with other Mediterranean countries. Oil, wine, pottery, and metalwork were the main exports.

Fishy business
Fishing provides a livelihood for many Greeks today just as it did in ancient times. This fisherman on the island of Mykonos is mending his nets.

Temple treasure
This clay pitcher with coins was found at the temple of Artemis at Ephesus. The coins, made of electrum, probably date from 650 to 625 BCE. The first coins were made in Lydia in Asia Minor (modern Turkey) in the seventh century BCE.

Coin showing the infant Herakles strangling snakes

Three coins
Each city-state issued its own coins. At first, they were made of electrum (a mix of gold and silver). Later coins were made of pure silver, or occasionally gold. Many were decorated with the symbols of Greek gods.

Coin showing Cyrus, the king of Persia

A tortoise coin from the island of Aegina

Into Africa
This pot in the form of an African head is evidence that the Greeks traded as far as the African coast.

Beasts of burden
Donkeys could negotiate narrow mountain tracks and carry heavy burdens.

Shoemaker

This painting of a cobbler is at the bottom of a red-figure cup. He is busy cutting and shaping strips of leather. Boots, sandals, and tools hang from the wall above him. This scene would have become visible to the drinker only when he had drained his cup.

At the loom

Upright looms, such as this modern one, were used to make clothing, drapes, and furnishing fabrics. Weaving was seen as a noble as well as a necessary task.

Blacksmith

This painting shows a blacksmith removing a lump of molten metal with his tongs. The brick furnace would have been fueled with charcoal and bellows were used to fan the flames.

Potter

Every Greek town had its potters' quarter (pp. 48–49) where pots were made and sold. On this wine cup, a potter sits at his wheel, which he controls with his knee. His pots sit on the shelf above him. Below, his pet dog (now slightly damaged) watches him work.

Deep seas

Wooden vessels, like this one, were used to fish in deeper waters, where a great variety of fish could be found. Salted fish and eels were Greek delicacies.

War

Warfare was part of Greek life, and the city-states frequently fought each other. In Athens, boys trained as soldiers from the age of 18. In Sparta, it was much earlier (pp. 56–57). Athenian soldiers were led by 10 commanders called *strategoi*. Infantry soldiers fought in close formations called phalanxes. Poorer soldiers served as archers or stone-slingers. The Greeks defended their empire with fast warships called triremes.

Shielded
This man holds his shield by passing his arm under an iron bar and gripping a leather strap.

Helmet with nose protection

Body armor

Greaves

Battle of Salamis
The sea battle of Salamis in 480 BCE was a turning point in the Persian wars. After this battle, the Persian king Xerxes went back to Asia, abandoning the invasion of Greece.

Speedy beasts
Greek chariots were often decorated with bronze figures of animals associated with speed.

Naked soldier
This naked warrior sits holding his body armor, spear, and shield. Nakedness was a symbol of bravery in Greek art.

Hoplite
Greek soldiers were called hoplites from the word *hoplon*, meaning shield. Only wealthy Greek men could become hoplites because they had to pay for their own weapons and armor.

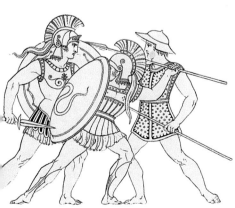

Foot combat

This vase painting shows two Greek soldiers separated by a herald.

Helmets

Helmets protected the head from blows and knocks. Some had crests made of horse hair to make the wearer appear more impressive and frightening.

Attic helmet has no nose guard

Corinthian helmet with long nose-piece and cheek guards

Breastplate

The breastplate, or cuirass, was usually made of bronze. It was designed to protect all the upper organs. Each cuirass was made to measure. The more expensive ones would have ridges that helped to deflect blows. The armor was made of two plates joined by leather straps. The sides of the body, therefore, were the most vulnerable.

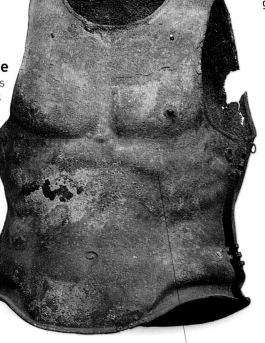

Sculpted ridges roughly aligning with chest muscles

Greaves

Hoplites wore bronze leg guards called greaves (below) to protect the lower part of their legs in battle. Some of these greaves may have originally been fixed on to large statues of heroic warriors in southern Italy.

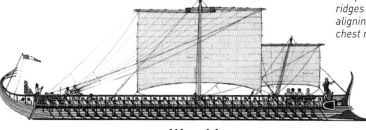

Warship

Greek triremes were powered by 170 oarsmen. The sailors sat in three levels, one above the other, on either side of the boat. At the prow was a pointed ram, coated in metal, which was used to sink enemy ships. The sails were probably made of linen and lowered when the ship was engaged in battle.

The long spear was the main weapon of the Greek infantry

Champion fight

This painting shows a fight between Achilles and Hektor, heroes of the Trojan War (pp. 12–13). Blood can be seen flowing from Hektor's leg. Both men are wearing the armor and crested helmets worn by infantry soldiers in the fifth century BCE.

The state of Sparta

Harbor battle
The Piraeus is the port of Athens. In this engraving, it is being besieged by Spartan ships in 388 BCE.

Sparta was founded in the tenth century BCE by the Dorians, who defeated the original inhabitants of the area. After long-running battles with their neighbors, the Messenians, the Spartans became a nation of warriors, dedicated to war. Their main rival was Athens. Boys of seven lived in army barracks and all Spartan men had to serve in the army. Noncitizens in Sparta were either *perioikoi* or *helots*. The *perioikoi* were free men who could trade and serve in the army. *Helots* farmed the land and did all the heavy work for their Spartan overlords.

Natural protection
This 19th-century German engraving shows the site of Sparta in Lakonia in southern Greece. It stood on a remote fertile plain, surrounded by mountains and the sea, which gave it natural protection from its enemies.

Ready for war
According to the Greek historian Herodotus, Spartan soldiers always combed their long hair before going into battle. The scarlet color of their military cloaks was a symbol of Spartan pride.

The Young Spartans
This painting by 19th-century French artist Edgar Degas (1834–1917) shows boys and girls exercising together. Sparta was the only Greek city-state to allow girls to take part in sports.

Spartan regime
The Spartan system of education, with its emphasis on physical fitness, was much admired in 19th-century Britain. Corporal punishment too was regarded as character-forming for schoolboys, just as it was in ancient Sparta.

Offerings
Hundreds of thousands of small figurines have been found at the sanctuary of Artemis on the banks of the Eurotas River in Sparta. The figurines were sold to visitors who often left them behind as offerings to the goddess. Once a year, Spartan boys were taken to this sanctuary to test their toughness and endurance.

Artemis

Warrior

Artemis

Figure playing pipes

A stag

In the lead
This girl is taking part in a running race. She is wearing a very short skirt that no girl from any other Greek city would be allowed to wear. Girls did not fight in wars, but they were trained to be fit and strong so that they would give birth to healthy sons who would grow up to be good soldiers.

Science and medicine

Asclepiades

Asclepiades was a famous Greek doctor in the first century BCE. He believed in the importance of compassion when treating his patients.

Ancient Greek scientists, influenced by Egyptian and Babylonian scholars, made great advances in biology, mathematics, and astronomy. In the third century BCE, the astronomer Aristarchus stated that the Earth revolved around the Sun, and Anaxagoras (500–428 BCE) discovered that the Moon reflected sunlight. An important area of Greek science was medicine. The Greeks thought that illness was a punishment from the gods and the sick would often visit the sanctuaries of Asclepius, the god of medicine. They believed he would prescribe treatments through his priests. The Greek physician Hippocrates (460–377 BCE) believed that illness had natural causes and based his treatments on detailed observations of the symptoms. Hippocrates is often described as the founder of modern medicine.

Antikythera mechanism

The inner workings of the mechanism were originally fronted by a brass plate with a dial that showed the positions of astronomical bodies

The different parts of the mechanism are all very corroded, and some are stuck together

The Antikythera mechanism

This device was found in a ship that sank in 82 BCE off the island of Antikythera. The complexity of its clocklike mechanism with its 30 gears stunned experts. X-ray analysis revealed that the device was probably an early type of "computer." When dates were entered via a crank, the mechanism indicated the relative positions of the Sun, Moon, and planets. It was most likely used for navigation, or perhaps for astronomical calculations.

It all adds up

This engraving shows the Greek mathematician Pythagoras (p. 46) working at an abacus and the Roman philosopher Boethius (480–524 CE) doing calculations.

Temple of Asclepius

In this engraving, people can be seen approaching a statue of Asclepius. His staff has a serpent twisted around it. A real snake (regarded as sacred) slithers on the plinth.

Temple visit

This 19th-century painting by John William Waterhouse (1849–1917) shows a mother and child at the temple of Asclepius. Priests of the god stand waiting to interpret his cure.

Thanks

Patients who had been cured by Asclepius often left a model of the part of their body affected by illness as an offering of thanks to the god. This marble relief of a leg has an inscription to Asclepius carved upon it and was dedicated by a worshiper named Tyche.

Hippocrates

Hippocrates (c.469–399 BCE) was born on the island of Kos. He wrote 53 books on medical topics, known as the *Corpus*. He taught that the human body was a single organism and that each part could only be understood as part of the whole.

ΑCΚΛΗ
ΠΙΩ
ΚΑΙ
ΫΓΕΙΑ
ΤΥΧΗ
ΕΥΧΑΡΙC
ΤΗΡΙΟΝ

Modern models

The practice of leaving a model of the affected part of the body as a thanksgiving, still continues in some countries. These modern examples are from Athens.

Tokens

People left these modern silver tokens of animals in the hope that they would be cured with the help of offerings.

Death and the afterlife

King of the Underworld
Hades (or Pluto) was the king of the underworld. Over time, the underworld became known simply as Hades.

Death came early for most people in ancient times, because life was harsh. Young men often died in battle and young women in childbirth. The Greeks had various ideas about life after death. The kingdom of the dead was thought to be underground, so many people buried their dead. Others cremated their loved ones on a funeral pyre. Greek tombs were decorated with pictures of feasts, and the body was buried with the dead person's favorite possessions and food for the afterlife. Many Greeks believed that the soul rose up to become one of the stars, waiting to be reborn in a new body.

The diver
This painting found on the inside of a stone sarcophagus (coffin) probably represents the leap of the dead into the unknown.

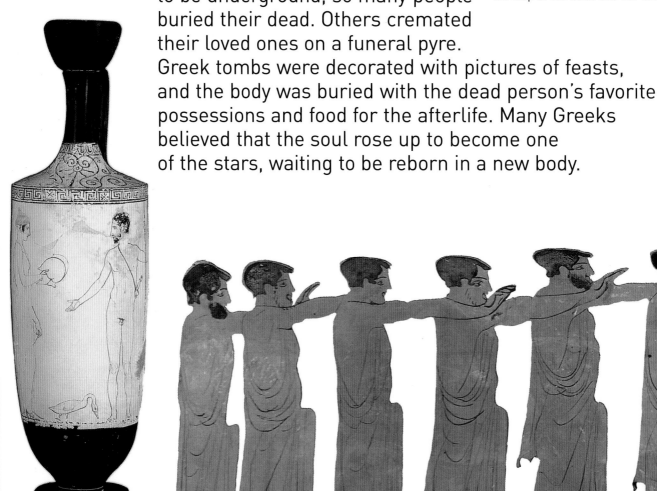

Flask of farewell
Offerings to the dead included narrow flasks known as *lekythoi*, which contained oil to anoint the body. They were usually delicately painted with touching scenes. This flask shows a dead warrior making his farewell.

Fare for the ferryman

This painting by John Stanhope (p. 13) is of Charon, the grim ferryman who carried the dead across the River Styx to the gloomy underworld. The one-way trip in Charon's boat cost one *obol*. The dead person's family sometimes left a coin on the body for the journey.

The entrance to Hades

Some Greeks thought that the steaming sulfur lake in Solfatara, southern Italy, was one of the entrances to the underworld.

Death before dishonor

After the Greek warrior Ajax failed to become the champion of the Greeks in the Trojan War, he killed himself by falling on his sword. This famous event is the subject of a play by Sophokles (p. 39).

Tombstone

In Athens at certain periods, tombstones carved in marble and painted in bright colors were placed above graves. Here, the dead man, Xanthippos, sits on an curved chair next to his children and his name is carved above him. He was a perhaps a shoemaker, since he is shown holding a foot.

Mourning line

A Greek funeral was a dramatic event. The body lay on a couch, with the feet facing the door to ensure that the spirit would leave. A procession of weeping mourners wearing black robes escorted the corpse. The women cut off their long hair as a sign of grief and gave a lock of it to the dead person.

Alexander the Great

Excavation at Ephesus
Ephesus was a city on the coast of Asia Minor where Greeks and many other nationalities lived together. The city thrived in the Hellenistic period.

In the fourth century BCE, Philip II turned Macedonia into the most powerful state in Greece. After he was killed in 337 BCE, his 20-year-old son Alexander took over. He conquered the whole of Greece, then took his army through Persia, Asia Minor, Egypt, Afghanistan, and India. He founded new cities and spread Greek culture far and wide. After his death in 323 BCE, the empire was divided up. The period from 323–330 BCE is known as the Hellenistic Age, from the word "Hellene," meaning Greek. The Hellenistic Age ended with the rising power of Rome.

Dog ring
On this ring from Hellenistic times, a shepherd sits with his dog and his crook.

Ruins at Pergamum

Aphrodite
Terra-cotta figurines of Aphrodite, the goddess of love and beauty, were popular in the Hellenistic Age. She is often shown fastening her sandal.

Ruins at Pergamum

Town planning
The wealthy Attalid dynasty lived in Pergamum, a Hellenistic city in Asia Minor. The ruins of their temples and other ornate buildings can still be seen on the terraces cut into the steep mountain site. The people of Pergamum would have had spectacular views over the surrounding area.

Eros tiara
Alexander's troops captured a great deal of Persian gold. At the front of this elaborate gold tiara is a tiny figure of Eros, the personification of love, holding a pitcher.

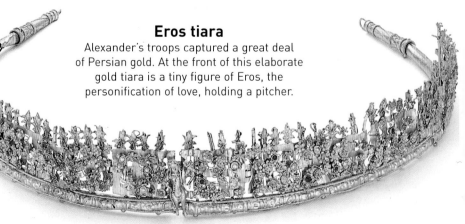

Alexander's empire

Alexander wanted to create a lasting empire. Many of his former soldiers settled in the colonies he founded and spread the Greek way of life. On the whole, Alexander treated those he conquered with respect. His conquests came to an end in India after his men refused to fight any farther.

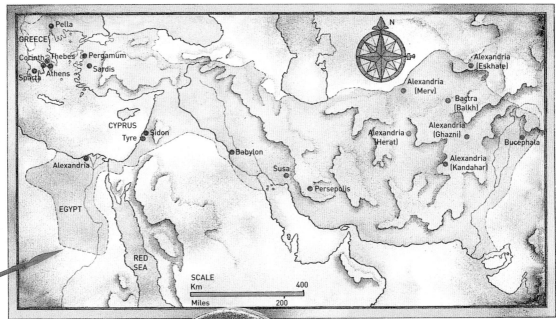

Trunk charger
This coin shows Alexander on horseback attacking two Indian warriors mounted on an elephant. It is thought to have been issued in Babylon in 323 BCE.

Richard Burton in the 1956 film *Alexander the Great*

The defeat of Darius
Alexander finally defeated the Persian king Darius III in a long and bloody battle at Gaugamela in Mesopotamia (southwest Asia) in 331 BCE. After Darius fled, Alexander called himself "King of Asia." This etching shows him fighting fearlessly on horseback.

Wall of fire
After defeating the Indian ruler Poros in 327 BCE, Alexander became a legendary figure in the East. This painting shows him building a defensive wall of fire.

Family of Darius
In this painting by the Italian artist Paolo Veronese (1528–1588), Alexander is accepting the surrender of the family of his defeated enemy Darius. The artist has dressed everyone in 16th-century clothes.

Did you know?

FASCINATING FACTS

Lion Gate, Mycenae, erected in the thirteenth century BCE

The Mycenaeans built such huge city walls—some were 46 ft (14 m) wide—that later civilizations believed they were built by giants.

The monumental proportions and one-foot-forward stance typical of *kouroi* (male nude temple statues) were adopted from ancient Egyptian figures.

Slaves were very important to the economy of ancient Greece. Some had very hard lives, but many were treated respectfully. Those taken prisoner by the Romans after their conquest were highly prized, and some worked as teachers and doctors.

Greek theaters, with their tiered seating, were specially built to enable the audience to see and hear the actors. They had to be carved into natural slopes, since the Greeks did not have the engineering skills to support the height and weight of theaters built on flat ground.

Archimedes, the famous mathematician and scientist, was murdered by the Romans in 212 BCE during their Greek conquest. This conquest was completed by 146 BCE.

Pan, god of the countryside, was believed to have a terrifying voice, which could paralyze animals with fear and topple city walls. His name gives us our word *panic*.

The apparently upright, tapering columns on the Parthenon actually lean inward slightly and bulge in the middle. This is to compensate for the effects of perspective, which visually distorts straight lines. Similarly, the building's base and steps are slightly higher in the middle than at the edges.

No mortar was used in the construction of Greek temples: stone blocks were fitted together and held with metal clamps and dowels.

The Greeks established a tradition of making and decorating pottery that lasted for more than 1,000 years. Some of their objects, such as the cups with pointed bases, might seem strange to us today. Others, however, such as the round pitchers and storage pots, are almost identical to the ones in a 21st-century kitchen.

Color was important to the ancient Greeks, especially in the Hellenistic Age (323–30 BCE). Many of the white marble statues from this time were once brightly painted.

Alexander the Great was given his horse Bucephalus at the age of 12. No adult could control it, but Alexander discovered that the horse was frightened of its own shadow, so he calmed him by turning his head to the Sun.

Greek god Pan playing a lyre

Macedonian soldiers originated a battle line called a phalanx. They would huddle together and form a compact mass with their shields. This powerful unit would then push and shove its way through enemy lines.

The Greeks invented picture mosaics in the fifth century BCE. They used this technique to decorate their floors with elaborate mythological scenes. The first mosaics were made from colored pebbles, but these were later replaced with specially cut cubes of glass, stone, or marble called *tesserae*, which produced finer detail and a larger range of colors.

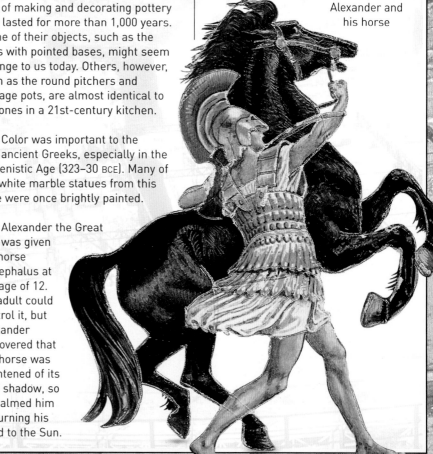

Alexander and his horse

QUESTIONS AND ANSWERS

Q What happened when the ancient Greeks consulted the oracle of Apollo at Delphi?

A Those who wanted advice from the oracle had to sacrifice an animal on the altar. They were then led to the priestess to ask their question. Although she was in a trance, the priestess answered questions clearly. Some replies were later turned into verses; these gave the oracle a reputation for giving confusing responses.

Q Why was Delphi considered a sacred place?

A According to myth, the god Zeus released two eagles from opposite ends of the Earth. Their paths crossed above Delphi, which established it as the center of the world. The god Apollo was thought to live at Delphi, which is why people came to the site to ask his advice.

Temple of Apollo at Delphi

Q Where did traditional Greek drama originate?

A Greek drama developed in the sixth century BCE from drama competitions during the festival of Dionysos. At first, people danced in groups and were often dressed as animals. Later, the actors wore masks with exaggerated features to indicate the characters they were playing. The first plays were tragedies based on myths and epic poems. Comedy did not appear on the Greek stage until about 480 BCE.

Q Where did the tradition of the marathon run come from?

A In 490 BCE, the Greeks were facing invasion by the Persians, whose ships landed in the Bay of Marathon. Although outnumbered, the Greeks surrounded the Persians and drove them back to the sea, losing only 192 men during the fighting, while 6,000 Persians died. News of the victory was taken back to Athens—a distance of 26 miles (41 km)—by a runner in full armor, who collapsed and died immediately afterward. This was the origin of the modern marathon.

Q Why is classical Greek architecture so widely admired?

A State and religious buildings in ancient Greece were designed to have perfect form and proportions. The classical style still remains popular today. Superb examples of buildings modeled on Greek architecture were built in Georgian England, revolutionary France, the newly formed United States, and 19th-century Athens (see pp. 68–69).

Record Breakers

FIRST OF THE GREATS
The Greek warrior Alexander (356–323 BCE) was the first leader to be widely known as "the Great." He founded 70 cities, several of which were named Alexandria after him.

EARLY LEARNING
Aristotle, a pupil of Plato, founded the Lyceum in Athens where subjects, such as biology and ethics, were taught. This institution turned Athens into one of the first university cities in the world.

FIRST STONE THEATER
The first stone theater ever built was the Theater of Dionysos, which was cut into the southern cliff face of the Acropolis. The remains of a restored Roman version can still be seen there today.

EARLY RECORDS
The first Olympic Games took place in 776 BCE. Originally, there was only one event—men's sprinting—and the runners were all local. Later, other competitions, such as wrestling, boxing, jumping, and riding, were added, and the games were opened to people from other parts of Greece.

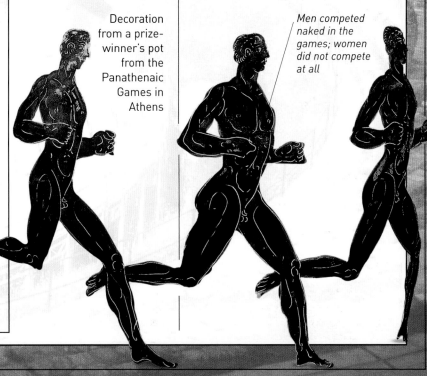
Decoration from a prize-winner's pot from the Panathenaic Games in Athens

Men competed naked in the games; women did not compete at all

Who's who?

Over a period of just a few hundred years, the civilization of ancient Greece produced an unequaled collection of statesmen, writers, artists, scientists, and philosophers whose ideas and innovations are still widely valued today.

STATESMEN

Solon
Athenian magistrate in the seventh and sixth centuries BCE. His legal, political, and economic reforms led him to be known as the father of democracy.

Themistokles
Leader of Athens and creator of the fleet that overpowered the Persians at the battle of Salamis in 480 BCE.

Perikles
Powerful Athenian general in the fifth century BCE. Perikles launched the extensive public building program that included the Acropolis.

Statue of Perikles

Alexander the Great
Born in 356 BCE, Alexander expanded the Greek empire into Persia, Asia Minor, Afghanistan, Egypt, and India before he died at age 32.

18th-century relief portrait of Alexander the Great

WRITERS AND ARTISTS

Pheidias
The most famous artist of the ancient world (he died around 432 BCE). He was celebrated for two giant statues, one of Athena and one of Zeus. Neither statue still exists. Today, he is best known for the Parthenon carvings, which he designed and supervised.

Aeschylus
One of the three major playwrights (with Euripides and Sophokles) writing in Athens in the fifth century BCE. A soldier who fought at Marathon, Aeschylus wrote nearly 90 plays, including *Prometheus Bound* and the *Oresteia*.

Euripides
Athenian playwright (left) who wrote controversial tragedies in the fifth century BCE, with themes of betrayal, murder, and injustice. Surviving examples of his plays include *Medea* and *Alcestis*.

Sappho
Poet who led a group of female writers on the Aegean island of Lesbos in the seventh century BCE. Sappho wrote mainly about family and friends.

Myron
Athenian sculptor of the fifth century BCE. Myron is best known today for his bronze statue *The Discus Thrower*, which survives only as Roman copies.

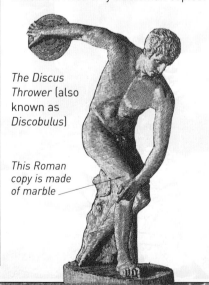

The Discus Thrower (also known as *Discobulus*)

This Roman copy is made of marble

THINKERS

Pythagoras
Philosopher and mathematician of the sixth century BCE who believed that the secrets of life lay in mathematics.

Herodotus
Historian of the fifth century BCE, known as the father of history, who produced the first written accounts of current events, such as the Persian wars.

Thucydides
Another historian of the fifth century BCE. He documented the Peloponnesian War between Athens and Sparta.

Socrates
Famous thinker of the fifth century BCE who produced no written work, but explored ideas through discussion. His talks, written down by his pupil, Plato, are known as "dialogues."

Plato
Pupil of Socrates who set up an Academy in Athens. Plato, too, believed in dialogues, and he produced two well-known works, *The Republic* and *The Laws*.

Aristotle
Pupil of Plato and founder of the Lyceum in the fourth century BCE. Aristotle had an outstanding gift for scientific observation. One of his most valued works is a treatise on ethics.

Epicurus
Greek philosopher of the fourth and third centuries BCE. He taught that genuine human happiness is the highest good. He wrote *On Nature* (a 37-volume work) and founded the Epicurean school of philosophy.

Socrates

SCIENTISTS

Hippocrates

Anaxagoras
Astronomer of the fifth century BCE who discovered that the Moon reflects light from the Sun.

Hippocrates
Founder of modern medicine in the fifth and fourth centuries BCE, Hippocrates created a code for the way doctors should behave, now known as the Hippocratic Oath. He believed all illnesses have a rational explanation.

Aristarchus
Astronomer of the third century BCE who understood that the Earth revolves around the Sun and that the Earth rotates on its own axis.

Asclepiades
Physician of the first century BCE who was compassionate in his treatment of patients. He believed in noninvasive treatments such as wine, massage, and bathing.

MODERN CLASSICISTS

Sir William Hamilton
Early 19th-century British diplomat and expert on Greek art. His collection of vases is now in the British Museum.

Heinrich Schliemann
German amateur archeologist who, in 1870, discovered the site of ancient Troy near the Turkish coast. This discovery supplied a factual basis for Homer's epic tales of the Trojan War.

Pierre de Coubertin
French aristocrat, who, inspired by the original Olympic Games, organized the first modern revival in Athens in 1896.

Sir Arthur Evans
English archeologist whose explorations at Knossos (Crete), starting in 1900, provided factual evidence of the Minoan civilization.

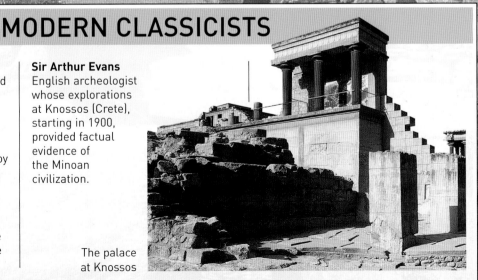

The palace at Knossos

Find out more

The influence of ancient Greece has spread throughout almost every country in the Western world. Perhaps the culture's best-known symbol is the fortified citadel of the Acropolis in Athens with its sacred center, the Parthenon. Completely symmetrical, the Parthenon was constructed of stone and white marble, an ideal medium for the detailed carvings on the frieze and portico. Today, its ruins are a popular tourist attraction for anyone with a fascination for the classical world.

The Parthenon
Completed in the mid-fifth century BCE, the Parthenon was designed by the architects Kallikrates and Iktinos to house a 40-ft (12-m) statue of Athena by Pheidias. Originally, its carvings were painted in blue, red, and gold.

Skillful carving gives an impression of great depth

The Parthenon frieze
The frieze that ran around the inner wall of the Parthenon was designed by the artist Pheidias. The individual segments of the frieze are called *metopes*. Together, they portray a procession of worshipers at the Panathenaic festival, held in Athens.

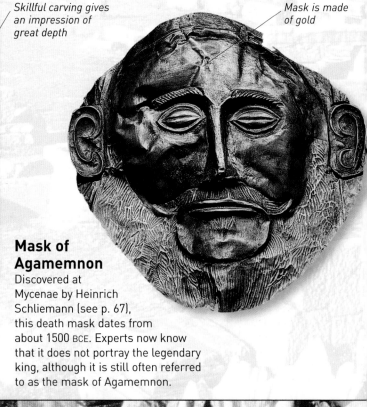

Mask is made of gold

Mask of Agamemnon
Discovered at Mycenae by Heinrich Schliemann (see p. 67), this death mask dates from about 1500 BCE. Experts now know that it does not portray the legendary king, although it is still often referred to as the mask of Agamemnon.

Greek theater
This drawing is of Creon, a character in Sophokles' play *Antigone*. Studying Greek theater helps us to understand more about classical Greek culture.

Harvesters hit the branches with sticks to knock the olives to the ground

Painted jar
Amphorae, two-handled vessels with narrowed necks, were designed to store liquid or foods preserved in liquid. The detailed scene on this jar suggests that it was used for olives or olive oil.

National Archeological Museum, Athens
Opened in 1891, this museum displays a vast number of Greek works of art. Designed in the Neoclassical style, the building's entrance is dominated by Ionic and Corinthian columns.

Marathon boy
Found on the seafloor, like many other Greek bronzes, this statue (in the National Archeological Museum, Athens) is thought to be the work of the fourth-century BCE sculptor Praxiteles.

PLACES TO VISIT

THE ACROPOLIS, ATHENS, GREECE
Although access is restricted to protect the temples, the Acropolis offers a unique collection, including:
- the Parthenon
- the Propylaia and the Beule Gate, historical entrances to the complex
- the Theater of Dionysos, birthplace of Greek tragedy, built in 342–326 BCE
- the Acropolis Museum, which displays a wealth of treasures from the site

ANCIENT DELPHI, GREECE
First excavated at the end of the 19th century, this site encompasses:
- the Sanctuary of Apollo
- the Castalian Spring, where visitors were required to bathe
- the stadium where the panhellenic Pythian Games took place

NATIONAL ARCHEOLOGICAL MUSEUM, ATHENS, GREECE
This is one of the world's most important Greek collections. Among its treasures are:
- the gold mask of Agamemnon
- superb examples of classical sculpture, including the Marathon Boy

METROPOLITAN MUSEUM OF ART, NEW YORK, NEW YORK
The museum's Greek and Roman galleries feature:
- a large collection of ancient vases
- important paintings and sculptures

BRITISH MUSEUM, LONDON, UK
One of the finest collections of Greek antiquities in the world. Look for:
- the Parthenon marbles (or the Elgin marbles)—sculptures and sections of the frieze brought to England by Lord Elgin in the 19th century
- a huge statue from the Mausoleum at Halicarnassus, one of the Seven Wonders of the Ancient World

THE GETTY VILLA LOS ANGELES, CALIFORNIA
Galleries are arranged by theme so visitors can view the artworks in the context of how they were used in classical society. Galleries include:
- Gods and Goddesses
- Stories of the Trojan War
- Dionysos and the Theater

Glossary

ABACUS Ancient counting frame made up of small beads threaded on wires.

ACANTHUS Plant with thick, scalloped leaves often seen in Greek art and architecture. The capital on a Corinthian column is covered with acanthus leaves.

Acanthus capital

AGORA Open market or public space in ancient Greece.

AMPHORA Two-handled jar with a narrow neck designed for storing wine, oil, or other liquid.

ANDRON Small dining room where men would entertain their friends at home.

ARYBALLOS Perfume pot, usually made of pottery. They were often in the shape of a fantasy creature or a real animal, such as a monkey or a hedgehog.

Colonnade

ASSEMBLY Gathering of people and officials who controlled public life in ancient Athens. There had to be at least 6,000 present to make an Assembly. (*see also* COUNCIL)

ATLANTES Carved male figure used as a column in classical architecture. (*see also CARYATID*, COLUMN)

CAPITAL The top section of a column. (*see also* COLUMN, CORINTHIAN, DORIC, IONIC, ORDER)

CARYATID Carved female figure used as a supporting column in classical architecture. (*see also ATLANTES*, COLUMN)

CHITON Item of clothing for both men and women in ancient Greece. *Chitons* were made from two rectangles of fabric fastened at the shoulders and down the sides, and tied at the waist. (*see also PEPLOS*)

CITY-STATE A conventional city that, with its surrounding territory, is also an independent political state.

COLONNADE Line of columns supporting a row of arches, a roof, or an upper floor.

COLUMN An upright structure used in architecture to support an arch, a roof, an upper story, or the top part of a wall. Most columns consist of a base, shaft, and capital. (*see also* CAPITAL, ORDER)

CORINTHIAN One of three main styles (orders) in classical architecture. Corinthian columns have bell-shaped capitals adorned with acanthus leaves. (*see also* ACANTHUS, DORIC, IONIC, ORDER)

COUNCIL Five-hundred strong advisory body that arranged the business of the Athenian Assembly. (*see also* ASSEMBLY)

CUIRASS Body armor, usually bronze, worn by Greek soldiers to protect their backs and chests.

DEMOCRACY A system of government in which the people being governed have a voice, usually through elected representatives.

DORIC One of the main styles (orders) in Greek architecture. Doric columns have wide fluting and a plain, round capital. (*see also* IONIC, CORINTHIAN, ORDER)

ELECTRUM A mixture of gold and silver used to make early Greek coins. Later coins were made of pure silver or gold.

EPINETRON Semicylindrical instrument used by Greek women to prepare wool for spinning. Often highly decorated, *epinetrons* fit over one knee.

In fresco painting, pigments are absorbed into wet plaster to fix their colors.

14th-century fresco prepared in a similar way to those of ancient Greece

FRESCO Wall painting applied to plaster when it is wet. (*see also* MURAL)

FRIEZE A deep band of decoration running along the upper part of a wall.

GALLEY Ancient Greek warship powered by one or more rows of oars.

GRAMMATISTES Teacher of subjects such as reading, writing, and mathematics. (*see also KITHARISTES, PAIDOTRIBES*)

GREAVES Bronze leg guards worn by Greek soldiers for protection in battle.

GRIFFIN Mythical creature with the head and wings of an eagle and a lion's body.

Griffin

GYMNASIUM Large room or building used for physical exercise.

GYNAECEUM Women's quarters in a Greek home.

HETAIRAI Group of women who sang, danced, played music, and entertained men at dinner parties.

HIMATION Outer cloak that was pulled under the right arm and draped over the left shoulder.

HIPPOCAMP Mythical sea horse with two front feet and a fish's tail.

HOPLITE Greek foot soldier, from *hoplon*, meaning shield.

IONIC One of three main styles (orders) in classical architecture. Ionic columns are slender, with narrow fluting and a scrolled capital. (*see also* DORIC, CORINTHIAN, ORDER, VOLUTE)

KITHARISTES Teacher of music. A *kithara* is much like a lyre, only larger. (*see also* GRAMMATISTES, PAIDOTRIBES)

KOUROS Marble statue of a naked boy, usually used as a cult statue.

KYLIX Shallow, footed drinking cup with two handles.

LABYRINTH Intricate and confusing network of passages formed by walls or hedges.

LYRE Stringed Greek instrument with a hollow body that was originally made from a tortoise shell.

MURAL Wall painting on dry plaster. (*see also* FRESCO)

OINOCHOE A decorative wine pitcher with a long neck, made either of pottery or metal.

ORACLE Sacred place where ancient Greeks could ask their gods, through a priestess, to give them advice or to foretell the future. The most famous oracle was that of Apollo at Delphi.

ORCHESTRA Flat, circular area where the actors and chorus performed in a theater.

ORDER One of several styles of classical architecture defined by shape and proportion. The three main orders are Doric, Ionic, and Corinthian (see p. 27). (*see also* CORINTHIAN, DORIC, IONIC)

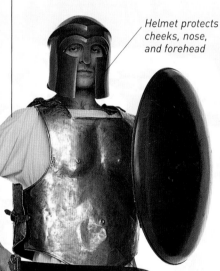

Early lyre with tortoiseshell body

PAIDOGOGOS Domestic slave responsible for accompanying Greek boys to school.

PAIDOTRIBES Teacher of physical, exercise, such as track or boxing. (*see also* KITHARISTES, GRAMMATISTES)

PALAISTRA Specially designed building, smaller than a *gymnasium*, with dressing rooms and a sand-covered courtyard where Greek boys were taught track and field and wrestling.

PEDIMENT Triangular gable end on a building, usually decorated with sculptures.

PEPLOS An early, simpler version of the Greek *chiton*.

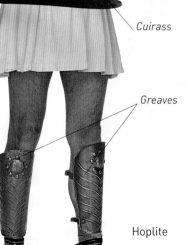

Helmet protects cheeks, nose, and forehead

Cuirass

Greaves

Hoplite

PYXIS Small container or casket in which Greek women kept cosmetics.

SLAVE Man, woman, or child who is owned by another person, usually to do work of some kind.

STOA Long, colonnaded structure with a wall on one side, where people met to talk and conduct business.

STRATEGOS One of 10 elected generals responsible for military decisions in Athens.

This structure was built around 200 BCE

Ruined *stoa* on the island of Lindos

SYMPOSIA All-male drinking parties, usually held in private homes.

THOLOS Round, domed building where the Council met. (*see also* COUNCIL)

TRIREME Fast warship powered by up to 170 oarsmen positioned over three levels on either side of the hull.

TYRANT Ruler of a Greek city-state who had usually seized power by force.

VOLUTE Spiral-like scroll used on Ionic capitals and on pottery vessels. (*see also* CAPITAL, COLUMNS, IONIC)

Index

Acknowledgments

Dorling Kindersley would like to thank:
The Department of Greek and Roman Antiquities, the British Museum for providing ancient artifacts for photography; Patsy Vanags of the British Museum Education Service for her assistance with the text; Bill Gordon for his superb model of a Greek farmhouse on pp. 28–29; Alan Meek for the armor & weapons on pp. 54–55. Helena Spiteri, Andrew Chiakli & Toby Williams for modeling the clothes & armor. Anita Burger for hairdressing & makeup; Jane Parker for the index. Dr. Hugh Bowden for assisting with revisions; Claire Bowers, David Ekholm-JAlbum, Sunita Gahir, Joanne Little, Nigel Ritchie, Susan St. Louis, Carey Scott, & Bulent Yusef for the clipart; David Ball, Neville Graham, Rose Horridge, Joanne Little, & Sue Nicholson for the wall chart.

For this edition, the publisher would also like to thank: Hazel Beynon for text editing, and Carron Brown for proofreading.

The publisher would like to thank the following for their kind permission to reproduce their images:
a=above, b=bottom, c=center, f=far, l=left, m=middle, r=right, t=top.

AKG-images: 66cra; Erich Lessing 64tl; **American School of Classical Studies, Athens**: 32cla; **Ancient Art & Architecture Collection**: 12tr, 44tl, 56cl, 63cr; R. Sheridan 58cl; **The Art Archive**: ET Archive 62crb; **Ashmolean Museum, Oxford**: 9tl; **Bildarchiv Preussicher Kulturbesitz (Antikenmuseum Berlin)**: 33tr; **The Bridgeman Art Library**: British Library 60tl; The Fine Art Society, London 13tl, 58br; House of Masks, Delos 20tl; Houses of Parliament, Westminster, London 18br; National Archaeological Museum, Athens 35cr, 50cr; National Gallery, London 56cb; Private Collection 30tl, 42br; Roy Miles Fine Paintings, Private Collection 61tl; Staatliche Antikensammlung und Glyptothek, München 46c; The Vatican Museums 47clb; **Corbis/Zefa**: 62c; Owen 25cl; Konrad Helbig 17c, 26tl; K. Scholz 19tr; Starfoto 50tl; **DK Images**: British Museum 16tr, 16bl, 16br, 17c, 17bc, 17br, 18tr, 19cla, 19clb, 19br, 20bl, 40tl 47tr, 47br, 48bc, 48br, 65tr, 65br, 67tr, 68clb, 69cla; Lin White 64tc, 64cr; **Ekdotike Athenon**: 52bl; **Getty**: Allsport/Gray Mortimore 45cl; Allsport/Vandystadt 45c; Hulton Archive 45b; Image Bank 51c, 52tl, 53br, 59bc; Time Life Pictures/Mansell 11tl, 12tl, 62tl; **Sonia Halliday**: 8tl, lite, 11tr, 12bl, 20tr, 25tl, 25tr, 25c, 33c, 44cr; **Michael Holford**: 6tr, 7tr, 9bl, 16tl, 20br, 21c; **The Kobal Collection**: 63c; **Mary Evans Picture Library**: 18tl, 26cl, 31cl, 35cr, 38tr, 39tl, 44b, 46tr, 46br, 47c, 47bc, 54c, 56tl, 56c, 56bl, 58tl, 58c, 58cr, 59, 63cb, 64br, 64bt, 69tc; **The National Gallery, London**: 9cr, 12br, 21tr, 22tr, 23bl, 63b; **Anne Pearson**: 24br; **Photo DAI, Athens**: (neg. Mykonos 70) 12cb;

Photostage: Donald Cooper 39tc; **Robert Harding Picture Library**: 38cl, 49br, 52bc, 53cla, 59bl; G. White 16cra; **Royal Ontario Museum**: 17tl; **Scala**: 11bc, 20cla, 26b, 35tl, 38b, 41b, 44cla; Delphi Museum 24bl; Heraklion Museum 8b; The Vatican Museums 36tl

Illustrations: John Woodcock and John Hutchinson.
Maps: Sallie Alane Reason

All other images © Dorling Kindersley. For further information see: www.dkimages.com